Praise for
HOLY DISOBEDIENCE

"*Holy Disobedience* is a visceral portrayal of a daughter's quest for the dark truth beneath the religious veneer of forced beauty and familial cover-ups. Melissa Duge Spiers bravely excavates her own coping mechanisms, cravings, and hauntings. But more than that, she persists until she identifies the wider context of the abuses in the Adventist church and a story that formed her upbringing before she was born. This riveting story is full of danger, sexually-charged energy, religious trauma, and vivid glamour; Spiers's writing is propulsive and intelligent as she calls out lies, enablers, and abusers—even when she's the one pushing herself to the extreme. I was rooting for her on every page, and her story will help set others free."

—Tia Levings, author of the *New York Times* bestselling *A Well-Trained Wife* and *I Belong to Me*

"In *Holy Disobedience,* Melissa Duge Spiers gives us an unflinching look at the toxic sludge that lies just beneath the surface of patriarchal, high-control religion. As she struggles to escape its quicksand, her journey of self-discovery moves from the superficial to the real and ultimately charts a path toward the freedom of her own self."

—Christa Brown, author of *Baptistland: A Memoir of Abuse, Betrayal, and Transformation*

"I laughed, I cried, I raged, and I cheered alongside the author. *Holy Disobedience* is a brave, penetrating memoir about spiritual abuse, bodily control, and the slow, defiant work of claiming autonomy. It offers something rare and necessary: language for the harm and a release to stop apologizing for surviving it. If you've ever been confined in the straitjacket of a faith that worships the appearance of goodness to cover its nefarious deeds, let this book grant you permission to rage until you break free."

—KATHERINE SPEARING, AUTHOR OF *A THOUSAND TINY PAPER CUTS*

"*Holy Disobedience* is a rare coming-of-age story lived twice: first within a high-control religion, and again after escape. With unflinching clarity, Melissa guides readers through deprogramming and self-discovery. Raw and courageous, these pages expose spiritual abuse, illuminate the shadowed history of Seventh-day Adventism, and transform inherited pain into power and advocacy. Her story grants readers permission to grieve their own losses without apology or the need to soothe others' discomfort. As she writes, 'I will no longer do pretty pain.'"

—STEPHANIE WARREN, WRITER AND PODCAST HOST OF *FOCUS ON YOUR OWN FAMILY*

"A pastor's daughter, Melissa Duge Spiers takes an unflinching look at the Seventh-day Adventist Church, a community that has escaped much scrutiny in the past century. Not only does Melissa vulnerably share the harm she experienced, but she also digs into the systemic and theological issues that have impacted countless like her. Compelling and insightful, this is an important addition to the growing genre of memoirs about high-control religion."

—CAIT WEST, AUTHOR OF *RIFT: A MEMOIR OF BREAKING AWAY FROM CHRISTIAN PATRIARCHY*

"I absolutely devoured this compelling book. In Melissa Duge Spiers's *Holy Disobedience,* she takes us on a harrowing journey through a secretive religious upbringing, the navigation of sexuality with no education, relationships rife with patriarchal control and violence, reckoning with dark family secrets, and a triumphant return to the safety of herself. Melissa is an incredible writer, and she expertly illustrates how high-control religions and religious purity culture prime women for abuse and silence. While exposing widespread and systemic abuse in the Seventh-day Adventist Church, she demonstrates great empathy and compassion even for those who cause harm. Melissa's writing is unexpectedly hilarious and warm, and I laughed out loud at times. Purity culture survivors won't want to miss this one, as stories like this have never been more urgent."

—Erica Smith, MEd, author of
The Purity Culture Recovery Guide and
creator of The Purity Culture Dropout™ program

HOLY DISOBEDIENCE

HOLY DISOBEDIENCE

Sex, Sin, and Secrets in the
Biggest Church No One Knows

MELISSA DUGE SPIERS

lakedrivebooks.com

Lake Drive Books
6757 Cascade Road SE, #162
Grand Rapids, MI 49546
info@lakedrivebooks.com

lakedrivebooks.com
@lakedrivebooks

Publishing books that help you heal, grow, and discover.

Holy Disobedience
Copyright © 2026 by Melissa Duge Spiers

All rights reserved, including the right to reproduce this book or portions thereof in any format whatsoever. No part of this publication may be reproduced or transmitted in any form or by any means, electronic or mechanical, including photocopying, recording, or any other information storage and retrieval methods, without the written permission of the publisher.

This book is a memoir. It reflects the author's present recollections and information gathering of experiences over time. Some of the names of individuals or institutions and their characteristics have been changed, some events have been compressed, and some dialogue has been recreated.

Paperback ISBN: 978-1-957687-73-5
E-book ISBN: 978-1-957687-74-2

Library of Congress Control Number: 2025928226

Cover and interior design by Laura Duffy Design
Author photo by Blind Owl Media

Dec. 2007

Dear Dr. Z,

Several years ago I stumbled across a newspaper interview in which you discussed recent abuse cases in the Seventh-day Adventist Church. It has taken me years to work up the courage to write to you.

...

I have no hope of getting the truth from the church or my family.

You, in a way, are the only person I can turn to.

Melissa S.

AUTHOR'S NOTE

The story contained within these pages is told to the best of my recollection. It is an honest effort to relate facts and experiences with candor but also kindness. Thus, names and details have been liberally adjusted in order to protect the privacy of everyone mentioned. We each behave differently in different relationships and situations, so my memories of events and interactions are not meant as immutable indictments of character—people change, grow, and respond in different ways.

FOREWORD

I've heard it said that being a former Seventh-day Adventist feels a lot like being marooned on an island: You're alone. How you survive is up to you to figure out by yourself. You see, Seventh-day Adventism isn't a church you just leave. You lose your entire support system, and even years after departing, many former members find that the church, its dogma, its secrets, and the specter of Ellen White still have their claws deeply embedded. To rephrase the classic adage, you can take the person out of Adventism, but you can't take the Adventism out of the person, at least not without great personal effort, therapy, and reprogramming, as I've come to find myself.

The pandemic, of course, only made the loneliness of deconversion more acute. As so many of us did, I turned to social media for community and connection. That's how I met Melissa, a fellow former Seventh-day Adventist who was also a writer, an advocate. She brought an all-around passionate, witty, and enjoyable presence to the space. We exchanged pleasantries and snarky banter over ex-SDA memes, fast becoming friends as we discovered we had even more in common: Each of our fathers had once served in church leadership. Each of them had also lost their position amidst scandal.

About a year ago I had the opportunity to interview Melissa for a podcast that I cohosted on leaving and deconstructing Seventh-day Adventism. What struck me most in that conversation, and in every conversation we've had since, was Melissa's ability to articulate the complicated, often contradictory emotions bound up in leaving a high-control religious group. She never overgeneralized the experience into either simple bitterness or triumph. Rather, she held space for the grief, the humor, the absurdity, the confusion, and the liberation that can all co-occur when a person finally steps outside the walls that once defined their entire world. That nuance can be a difficult thing to grasp, and it's also essential for healing.

Melissa's story is a compelling testament that does just that, resting in the tension of healing that can happen even amid half-answers and institutional silence. In a climate where former Adventists often feel pressured to either justify their exit, soften their story for the comfort of others, or just fade away altogether, Melissa speaks with clarity, wit, and unapologetic honesty. Courageous honesty. She does not shy away from discussing the Adventist pattern of institutional coverups when dealing with abuse and the human toll this leaves behind. As many former Adventists know, the church is notorious for being quite litigious, rarely hesitating to pursue legal action when its reputation is at stake. Too many stories have been silenced by non-disclosure agreements and non-disparagement clauses. This makes Melissa's story all the more vulnerable *and* valuable.

If leaving Adventism is to be marooned alone on an island, then this book is the first friendly ship on the horizon. Melissa doesn't merely recount her own experience; she names the patterns, the doctrines, the psychological residue, and the generational echoes that shape life inside and beyond Adventism. She delves into the fear, the indoctrination, the way a belief system can covertly guide your inner world long after you've stopped attending the church. She also writes with profound tenderness for the people we once were—the kids who learned so young that their bodies were bad, the teens yearning to get out and find freedom, the adults striving for healing while still being haunted by the stark warnings of a long-dead prophetess.

Healing from Adventism, or any high-control religion, isn't a straight path. It comes in waves: moments of anger, clarity, unexpected nostalgia, and wrestling with the past. What Melissa gives readers here is not a map but a shared language. She validates the messy middle, the unresolved questions, and the slow reclamation of one's identity. She reminds us of what it takes to not only look at our painful past, but to move on from it. Her book is a testament that healing doesn't require perfection or even all the answers, only the courage to tell the truth.

—ANDREW KERBS, TRAUMA RESOLUTION COACH,
CO-HOST OF *SUNDAY SCHOOL DROPOUTS*

PROLOGUE

With my face pressed heavily into the bed, I grit my teeth, squinting one eye like a cyclops to make out the words printed in script across the sheet: *je me souviens*. "I remember."

More words rise from the pattern on the 400-thread-count French fabric in which I wrap myself every night. The rhythmic motion of my naked body being driven over the cotton makes them jump in and out of focus, appearing and disappearing in disjointed phrases. *Le monde . . . comme il faut.*

I like sleeping in words, even poorly written nonsense on overpriced sheets calculated to make their purchasers feel exclusive and well traveled. The sheets are my Paris, my secret escape, a reminder of the path not taken, a throwback to remind me of those few short years in which I had truly escaped and had a life of my own.

Très cher . . . Mon Dieu. Funny thing, that great and fearsome Dieu of my childhood. While I was certainly *ton*, God had never seemed to be *mon*. But look at me now, how free I am, spread out here in pain.

When my parents once stayed in our guest room on these sheets, my father pointed out that things printed with French phrases reeked of yuppie pretentiousness, of trying too hard, like the fancy "Chaud" and "Froid" faucet handles my husband, Andrei, and I had special-ordered for our guest bathroom. "Now, Meliss," my father chortled, eyes twinkling, "you realize, don't you, that a real European would never have these sheets!"

I agreed with him, as I always did. My dad was the most brilliant, erudite person in my hemisphere. But I needed the sheets to remind me of those few good years, of that path not taken and now gone forever.

"Daddy," I gasp, crushed into the expensive memory foam mattress.

I wish the mattress could remember everything so I could forget. I grab *les bonnes rêves* and crumple them in my hand as the commotion above and behind me becomes more insistent: harder, deeper, faster.

I free my hand from where it is pinned at my side and slide it along the sheets—*douce, aime, nuit*—until I can bring it to my mouth. I part my lips slowly and begin to suck my thumb, caressing it with lips and tongue. Physically it soothes and numbs me. It also increases the frenetic pumping and grinding behind me, which is soothing too, because it means I will soon be free.

I close my eyes—*torride, très gentile*—and I suck slowly and rhythmically. I know what I need to do.

"Mmmmm, Daddy, yes, yes, please . . . please, Daddy, please," I whisper.

I cannot look at the lovely words on the sheets anymore. If I can just get through this, I won't have to think about it again for a few days.

It's very simple, I tell myself. It works every time.

"Yes, Daddy, please. More."

My words are slobbery and lisping, wrapped around my thumb. The sheer monotony of the performance blends with the pain to form a dull film in my brain. The print goes out of focus.

"Deeper, Daddy, give me more." I can barely speak, but I will myself to relax as the frenzy reaches its apex.

There are two or three more excruciating thrusts and an interminable pause.

Andrei finally releases me and I can breathe once more. My husband is pleased for another day or two.

I slowly ease open my balled fists, releasing the crushed sheet that had wetly accompanied my thumb. I idly wonder which words had been put in my mouth—what silent, cottony verbiage I had been choking on.

I open my eyes.

Je ne me souviens pas: I don't remember.

A full decade later, I am still trying to remember. I really am.

"What are your feelings about sex?" the dowdy woman across from me asks.

I stare at her.

Je ne me souviens pas.

Andrei and I are in marriage counseling at this point—together for eleven years, married for four—and I really love my smart, shy husband. He has morphed over the years from poorly dressed martial arts teacher to sharp-tongued VP at a major company. We are much alike in many ways: sarcastic, misanthropic, bookish, ambitious. And we take our relationship seriously—sex issues and all.

I don't remember how we found her, but the therapist's office is in an old church. It is the first time I have been to a marriage counselor, of course, but it is also the first time I have been back inside a church since I fled my childhood religion.

I don't care for the therapist, but I love marching under the prim steeple, making a solemn procession through the carved double doors and into a former Youth Group room to spew details of sexual deviance all over the carpet like a sorority initiate after a hard night. I know the truth of what happens so often within walls like these, so each sordid revelation I vomit up is a small strike back.

"What sexual fantasies do you have?" the woman asks in her

best impartial, unable-to-be-shocked voice.

I want out of my marriage. Does that count as a sexual fantasy?

In the face of my mute stare, she presses on. "When did you begin to dislike the sex?"

I blink hard. Had I ever *liked* the sex? I needed it. Wasn't that the same thing?

Andrei is glued to my side on the couch, swollen eyes imploring me to say something he wants to hear. He squeezes my fingers in desperation until they turn numb.

If the sex had stayed simply violent and degrading, we might not be sitting across from the gray-haired therapist with the smoker's voice and the African masks on her walls. But over the years, it has become apparent that Andrei isn't into rough so much as roleplay, and after the initial frisson of varied sexual ferocity, we have settled into rote repetition, our roles in and out of bed similarly ritualized. Andrei has grown increasingly self-serving, controlling, and smothering in every arena. After so many years, we have become conjoined twins—but my side has all the vital organs. And they're starting to fail.

"Okay, let me rephrase that," says the therapist, betraying an unprofessional hint of frustration as my silence drags on. I am not being purposely difficult; I am *never* purposely difficult. I just don't feel I have anything to offer on the subject. Gauging my own sexual interest is an unfamiliar sport.

She tries once more. "When did you like the sex?"

Did I ever like it?

My search for rough sex has lasted forever. Even before I discovered *Blue Velvet* and the *Story of O*, I was goading bewildered preppies to hit me and hurt me, urging them to inflict bruises, welts, and bites. I didn't know why. I don't know if I ever knew why, and I didn't care. I always told myself that it is just what I like.

Not all of my conquests allowed me to bully them into violent sex, of course, but none of them lasted very long. I had no long-term relationships before Andrei. For those glorious short years of freedom, I had always moved quickly from one hookup to the next, looking for something, searching for someone.

Something to make me *feel*. Someone to make me feel *bad*.

At last the counselor has something to work with. She removes her glasses and lowers her chin, gazing at me with the mixture of sympathy and reprimand I used to get from my high school calculus teacher. "Why does sex have to make you feel bad? Where did you learn that sex is bad?"

I attempt to return her gaze steadily, but my face does not cooperate. The corners of my mouth leap in lopsided, disconnected lurches, like Venetian blinds in a cheap hotel room: first one side, then the other, jerking uncontrollably upward in drunken, goofy spurts.

Clearly, she does not know the Seventh-day Adventist Church.

1

I was raised a strict Adventist, as was every member of my family reaching back four or five generations. The fifth richest church organization in the world, with a reported material net worth over $15 billion and a global membership of 25 million and counting (a larger organization than either the Mormons or the Southern Baptists), the Seventh-day Adventist Church is the biggest religion no one has ever heard of.

Founded in 1863 by "prophet" Ellen G. White, who suffered a devastating head injury in childhood that left her with lifelong seizures and hallucinations which she interpreted as mandates from God, the church rapidly expanded within just a few generations from a fringe end-times cult (one with a particular fixation on the evils of everything sexual and Catholicism) into a sprawling, high-control, fundamentalist denomination with a formidable worldwide presence.

A formidable yet mostly hidden presence. Despite quietly administering the second largest private education system and third largest healthcare system in the world and spawning the likes of David Koresh, The Ant Hill Kids, Ben Carson, Colin Cook, Prince, Little Richard, Usain Bolt, Black Sabbath, and more than a few serial killers, the Seventh-day Adventist Church has remained unbelievably successful at staying completely under the radar and out of the news.

Fostering an all-encompassing secrecy from the outset, it is a sect built on singular insularity. With Adventist-run schools, businesses, food manufacturers, television and radio studios, magazines, publishers, and radio channels, it is quite possible (and, for practitioners, preferable) to live one's entire life like a sanctified veal calf: folded within the Adventist box, real-world muscles atrophying, no contact with or exposure to outside of that box. Anyone who strays from the fold is game for all manner of coercive agents who deploy methods ranging from subtle shaming to exorcisms, forced counseling, prayer circles, shunning, and guilt trips.

Tactics of increasing membership through mission work and outreach are hardly less draconian yet equally suspect. While North American membership has stagnated from the mid-twentieth century onward and is now reportedly shrinking, the church has only expanded its reach worldwide through an aggressive colonial-missionary approach. Destitute or at-risk peoples in both developing countries and the US are flooded with generosity: medical treatment, English lessons, health seminars, vegetarian cooking classes, stop-smoking clinics, hospitals, and schools, all accompanied by the often not-so-subtle expectation of attendance at associated religious seminars, baptisms, and services. It is an extraordinarily effective way of swelling church ranks and guaranteeing generations of grateful and obedient Adventists like those on both sides of my family.

Like so many, both my paternal and maternal great-grandparents and grandparents—poor but ambitious—were lured in by the dangled mix of educational advancement and medical training. Nearly all of the males on both sides of my family doggedly worked their way through the Adventist school system, earning their way to the pinnacle of Adventist academic achievement: degrees from the world-renowned Loma Linda Medical School in Southern California. It was a shrewd and eventually very lucrative gamble on the part of the church, taking in and educating these destitute young men, as my entire family through several subsequent and quite affluent generations have been devout tithe-paying Adventists ever since.

My father, whose parents pushed him several years ahead of his class and sent him away to Adventist boarding high school at the age of ten or eleven, initially deviated from the family's physician tradition and chose to pursue a PhD in physics at a major non-Adventist University. However, in a dramatic and mysterious about-face only weeks into his program, he fled across the country to the Adventist seminary. Thus he was serving as an Adventist youth pastor and leader of a Pathfinder group (an Adventist imitation of Scouts with a faux military veneer) when I was born, the second of two girls, in the arid, ugly Central Valley of California.

Everyone loved Dad. People gravitated to him, turned their faces up adoringly when his distinctively deep, crackling voice boomed from the pulpit. Dad's sermons were exciting: stories of Bible wars, dramatic migrations and terrifying enemies vanquished, instead of the usual dull parsing of verses, pious espousing of righteousness, and "call to Jesus" humdrum. No matter how often or where we moved, Dad's star power drew people in, and together he and Mom gave off a distinctly Jack-and-Jackie vibe: stylish and charming, with good looks to spare. They were special, and they made me feel special.

That was a little bit of needed armor when it came to always being the new kid. Because we moved a lot. Later, people would ask if I was an army brat, and I would laugh and say, "No, a medical brat." Our peripatetic family life started when Dad was a youth pastor, during which time we moved churches suddenly and repeatedly, but soon enough my dad made yet another abrupt about-face and left the ministry to pursue the "family business": an MD. We bounced around from place to place as he completed medical training and residencies in various parts of the Midwest.

When I was young, moving was not as traumatic for my sister and me as it might have been for normal kids, however. From our earliest memories we already knew we weren't normal. We weren't even normal for Adventist kids. There were no sleepovers or playdates. We did not have friends outside of Sabbath School (the child-centered pre-church services we attended each Saturday). We were not allowed to join Pathfinders or attend Vacation Bible School or go to Adventist sleepaway camp. There was a great lurking, intangible danger out there somewhere that could only be avoided by keeping us at home, always in Mom's sight. We interpreted it as slightly biblical, probably our fault, surely the shortcoming of something or someone else, and definitely something mysterious and sinister that floated, omnipresent, unspoken, just out of reach.

In obedience to the prophet Ellen White's edicts, we were homeschooled by my mother through early elementary school, a stilted and agonizing process for all of us. It was all part of our tightly monitored and disciplined upbringing, as Ellen advises, "Mothers, be sure that you properly discipline your children during the first three years of their lives. Do not allow them to form their wishes and desires. The mother must be mind for her child." There were no homeschool groups or support systems at that time, either within or outside of the church; homeschooling was an extreme, freak-fringe activity, so we had no school friends or activities. All three of us chafed under the dry formality of the arithmetic and grammar drills in ancient looseleaf binders that we were duty bound to complete and mail in each week. Math was particularly difficult for me, the endless bouts with arithmetic flash cards sending me into angry tears and Mom into frustrated rages.

She did not have to teach me to read, however.

2

"P_{ee} . . . nusss . . ."

I am three years old.

"Pennn . . . iz . . ."

I dive over the back window railing of our VW van headfirst onto the scorching red leather bench seat, squirming upright to settle in next to the miserable pretty girl with the fascinating papers fluttering beside her. It is before seatbelts and car seats, and my sister and I habitually ride wild in the theater-stage back window box of the van, rolling around on our stomachs staging Breyer horse and Barbie scenes. But today the silent teenager and her untouched, lurid, cartoon-drawing brochures are much more interesting. Clutching my plastic palomino, cruising over the text, I sound out the words over and over. "Peenussss!"

I am very proud of myself. It is a mystery to everyone how I have learned to read. More remarkable than my age is the fact that we have hardly any children's books in the house. Where did I learn? And we certainly have nothing that looks like this, with graphic displays of spread legs and line-drawn vaginas disgorging hairy infant crowns.

"SurV1X!"

I can feel the pretty girl beside me shrink away. I want her to like me. I want to impress her. I need to please people. Anyone, everyone. I rush to try again.

"Plakenta . . ."

The silence is as oppressive as the inland empire heat that hangs in our van. The air conditioning broke years before.

Something is very bad. Maybe I'm just pronouncing it all wrong.

"Plasssenta?"

Something is definitely very absolutely totally not okay.

At three I already know the weight of both my imperfections and the mandate that I must not ruin it for everyone else in Heaven. Ellen White said so! "But wicked children God does not love. He will not take them to the beautiful City, for he only admits the good, obedient, and patient children there. One fretful, disobedient child would spoil all the harmony of Heaven." I already know all sins carry the same weight. Whether it's being disobedient or reading the wrong thing, I might mess it all up for everyone forever.

I am paralyzed with fear, shivering in spite of the heat.

Our beloved VW van eventually grew old and decrepit after we fled California for the ugly Midwest, the gray, slushy winters so drab compared to our sunny SoCal memories. During my elementary school years the entire center floorboard slowly rusted out in the salt and snow of harsh winters. Even when a piece of plywood was laid over the growing hole, random jets of freezing black slush would occasionally shoot over us kids huddled in the back seat.

But that would be nothing compared to the icy looks shooting into me now through the rearview mirror from my mother, high up in the driver's seat, posture rigid. Unbeknownst to me, she is grimly fulfilling one of the youth pastor's wife's least comfortable obligations: ferrying unwed mothers-to-be to doctor's appointments. These young women are important church catches in the BOGO missionary tradition, a repeat of the method used to snag my paternal great-grandmother: seduce the vulnerable young mother with financial support and medical care, and you get not just one, but two—or more!—meek and indebted new church members.

The particular unfortunate specimens like the unwed girl beside me are an even more secure prize than my proper, widowed great-grandmother. These girls are the fallen fornicators, the tawdry tramps whose sign of sin grows more visible every month. It is always their fault, regardless of whether it was ever their choice, and it is everyone's Christian obligation to make sure they feel their unworthiness. They are taken in by the church ladies and showered with equal parts solicitude and shame, guaranteeing at least two generations or more of grateful, appropriately cowed members who will forever struggle to distinguish disgrace from duty, obligation from devotion.

"Vagg . . . vajjjeena . . ." My earnest, lispy repetitions continue to taunt the unfortunate girl and enrage my mother, but I am safely out of her reach. She cannot rip the pamphlet away from me, viciously slapping my hands like she does when I pull at the clips and pins of my Sabbath church hairdos. So she seethes impotently, shooting looks into the rearview mirror that terrify me and the girl beside me.

Even though they are right beside her, the unhappy pretty girl won't touch the papers. She will not acknowledge this bomb I have unwittingly detonated. She seems paralyzed now. I shrink alongside her. I feel her humiliation, I feel my mother's fury, and I wonder what I have done that is so very, very wrong.

It has something to do with what I am reading, this fascinating display of babies and bodies and breasts, nakedness and nipples, penises and penetration. I am too young to understand, but I am old enough to know I cannot ask. Whatever this is, it is a huge, forbidden, hidden subject. It is saturated in shame, anger, fear, disgust. It is big. And it is very, very bad.

3

I buried the subject deep within me, but my search for reading material went on unabated. While I apparently could find sex education pamphlets in the back of our VW bus, the usual childhood materials were forbidden in our house. There was no Dr. Seuss, no Berenstain Bears, no Sesame Street, no fairy tales or Hardy Boys or Nancy Drew. Dear Ellen White had decreed that fiction was a waste of time and weakened the mind, that all material consumed should be holy and "instructional." That seemed to sit well with my mother, who was short on imagination, playfulness, and silliness. She had never been a reader.

My father, on the other hand, was an inveterate reader in half a dozen languages, his library regularly commanding the largest room or two in every house we inhabited, and from my first memories I yearned to be just like him, craving a bookish, intellectual life. But his book overflow somehow did not affect our childhood reading selection, which remained one sad shelf half stocked with ancient, yellowing biographies of not very interesting people, science experiment manuals from my father's youth, and the random baby book about puppies or the *Little Red Hen*. The only novels were a well-worn set of *Little House on the Prairie* volumes, which passed muster as part history and part instructional manual for pious, frugal living.

There was at one point a forgotten old illustrated volume of *Grimm's Fairy Tales* that, when I was discovered reading it, was yanked away with great indignation. Too violent, too scary, too full of the supernatural and make believe. It was thrown scornfully into the trash so that our focus could return to the wholesome Bible tales that we inhaled from Arch Books: catchy, rhyming Bible story paperbacks that we could parrot from memory. The saucy, poetic language and Disney-like illustrations were the sweet coating on the pill, helping us suck down stories about Jacob's brothers selling him into slavery and Samson falling prey to Delilah. We would squeal and chant along with whichever parent was reading to us as Daniel was thrown into the lion's den, Meshach and company were thrown into fire, and Jonah was swallowed by a giant cetacean.

There were a few missionary tales of brave white Adventists entering scary foreign countries full of Satan worshippers, battling curses and demonic possessions and needing exorcisms so terrifying that I wet my bed in fear every night. And there was a compendium of *Uncle Arthur's Bedtime Stories*—patronizing, moralistic tales in which the paralyzing loss of a mother, father, sibling, pet, or grandparent was always tied to the transgressions of a child: lying, bragging, laziness, not doing their chores, and the biggest sin of all, *being disobedient*. Failing to blindly indulge, pacify, and placate someone in authority always ended in disaster for these sinful children. Godly children instantly, unquestioningly obeyed everyone and anyone's commands. Uncle Arthur made sure we hyperventilated at night from toddlerhood onward, quaking over our bad actions, terrified into always being nice, never saying no, and desperately submitting to every source of authority lest we be the ones to ruin *all* of Heaven through our insufficient obedience.

I avoided as long as possible the writings of Ellen White: dull, dry, bewilderingly circuitous publications that cannibalized themselves gratuitously. For family worship we read her biblical history books, full of scary wars between God and the Devil and a bewildering number of ways humans were sinful, damned, and judged. Particularly terrifying were her warnings of end-times persecution when the Catholics would institute a worldwide "Sunday Law," under which we would be torn from our parents, forced to flee to the mountains, and live out our time as God's Remnant being hunted, tortured, and killed for our faith. Dad's collections of her entire writings, heavily highlighted and underlined, were in constant rotation on his reading pile, and her *Child Guidance* and *The Adventist Home* were Mom's instruction manuals. So even though her prophecies terrified me into wetting the bed for years and launched my lifelong battle with chronic insomnia, I still dearly wanted to revere Ellen too. But as much as I tried, the endless catalog of wrong behaviors, attitudes, and even thoughts felt like constant mental spanking, and I had enough of the real kind to deal with, thank you very much.

Our household discipline model combined the religious parenting advice, "Spare the rod, spoil the child," a generally dehumanizing view of children, and White's exhortation that children are born and remain evil until they can make a full acceptance of Jesus at around age twelve. Until then, their full demonic nature must be trained, beaten, punished, intimidated, or manipulated out of them. This view was further pushed by the James Dobson books littering my parents' shelves on breaking the will of children and Christian patriarchy's blind-obedience culture: "Obey all the way, right away, in a happy way." Expressing individual wants and needs was not an option, nor was ever saying no.

It all blended together with a long matriarchal tradition in our family in which Mom asserted complete, frenzied dominion over everything in our lives, with particular attention to our looks. Beginning with our toddler bodies, our only value was in looking and being "pleasing" and attractive at all costs in order to be worthy of love from Church and God and Men. Borrowing blindly from her own mother, mine insisted a lot of her draconian rules about our looks were because "Your father likes it when you're pretty," something that made me feel deeply icky and stirred skepticism and outrage: it never came from Dad himself. But there was no questioning any of it. Just swallow and obey, all the way, right away, in a happy way, or risk a slap, a belting, or worse.

Saturday morning church preparations were an especially excruciating and stressful time, with my sister and I forcibly transformed into doll-like creatures. There was a joyless, frantic brutality to Mom's beauty mandates. No enjoyment or celebration of being beautiful, just a grinding obligation to shut up, gussy up, and then be humble about it. Dad was mysteriously not in the picture. He was rarely around any time, but particularly not while my angry, wound-up mother forced us into tights and ruffles and beehives.

Of particular interest was our hair: a raw point from my mother's own upbringing that she furiously handed down to us. Her own mother, who flaunted a luxurious and perfectly wavy Cruella de Vil coif, had never failed to mock Mom's weak hairline and thin, straight hair. In turn, Mom constantly reminded us of our misfortune in having her "ugly, stringy, straight hair." In order for it to be deemed beautiful—and thus us deemed acceptable—it had to "hold a curl." A very specific Goldilocks curl: not too tight, not too stringy, not too frizzy.

Wildly out of step with the 1970s hippie, long-haired aesthetic at the time, our unwilling strands were painstakingly twisted and shellacked every Sabbath into Shirley Temple sausage rolls, gigantic stiff buns, bubble bangs, French twists. But even those excruciating and drawn-out styling sessions—after an uneasy night on lumpy curlers that tore hair and poked skin with every toss and turn—paled in comparison to the tortures of the underlying requirement: the home permanent.

4

I wind my fingers tightly into the deep shag carpet, holding on as if my life depends on it. Our grandfather always threw coins onto this carpet when he visited, grinning as we scrabbled around to find the riches. But now it is not a playground; it is my only hope. I swear I will hold on until the fibers rip or my fingers are torn off.

Tears threaten, but I choke them back, trying not to make a sound. Mom has been telling us for weeks it is time for a permanent again. Today, I refused. Screwing up my eight-year-old courage, I told her I was simply not going to submit to the hated procedure anymore. And then I hid, right here under my bed, crying and shaking.

My attempts to escape are pathetic as there is no way out of the room I share with my sister, and even if I had the courage and presence of mind to lock the door, I couldn't. All locks are disabled in our houses, always, even on the bathroom door. Everything is fodder for unexpected or forcible entry, except for Dad's office door, behind which he famously retreated and locked Mom out early in their marriage. It is where he inevitably retreats every six months or so, like right now, when the Toni Cold Crème battle begins.

My mother is infuriated, she's screaming. "Just how do you think you are going to keep a curl in your hair? It doesn't hold a curl by itself!" She commands me to come out. She bellows, she threatens. She lies down on her stomach and fishes for me viciously.

Mom is acidly critical of anything and everything about any and every female alive, young or old. Little girls with binkies; teenagers in clogs or faded jeans; old women with thick waistlines;

tired mothers wearing no makeup; any woman too vivacious, outspoken, educated, ambitious, competitive, overdressed, underdressed, sloppy, showy, simply "too" anything—they are all fair game for Mom's constant judgment.

We have come under that same scrutiny from babyhood onward. Our personalities, energies, moods, and expressions are all scornfully managed; nothing but compliant, happy submission is allowed. Yet none of it is as important as our looks, and nothing on that front is as offensive as our ugly hair. In Mom's book there is no such thing as beautiful straight hair, and our duty is to be beautiful at all costs.

The costs are so miserably high. They are exacted not only with the constant criticism but with physical force. We are hit for resisting the perms, slapped for pulling out bows, barrettes, and clips on our dreaded spit curls, those crusty spirals pasted on our cheeks with Mom's saliva and pinned in place until the unbearable itch of drying stops.

The most important values in my eight-year-old life right now are "holding a curl" and obeying both the heavenly father and our earthly one, who is God's representative on this sinful planet. It is all jumbled together. It all makes me feel "creepy icky" and suspicious.

Right now I don't feel creepy icky, though; I feel the pain of rug burn as my mother drags me out from under the bed where I have been sobbing into the dust bunnies. Her fingers dig into my arm, bloodshed avoided only by the Adventist shunning of long, painted manicures, and I am forced—blubbering, bruises welting up on my arms—into the kitchen and onto a tall stool. There I remain, sniffling, shivering, for a solid hour as my long hair is sectioned into wafer-thin noodle strips, wound on dozens and dozens of plastic rollers, and cinched down so tightly my scalp grows numb.

Torture begins afresh with the pungent smell of ammonia,

burning my eyes and coating my throat with a gunky sting. The cold liquid oozes down over the rollers and into the cotton wadding looped around my head, bending my ears out at a weird angle. And then it really begins: the confirmation that my scalp is indeed not numb as the caustic chemicals turn from clammy drips into allover fire ant gnawing.

Hot tears track down my face. My nose begins to run, both from the burning smell and the emotional destruction. But I cannot sniffle; I cannot make a sound, or I'll be found out.

It's too late. I am jolted forward—the harsh crack echoes before I even feel it—Mom hits me twice, hard, between the shoulder blades with the back of her paddle brush. "Nobody wants to hear you acting selfish and miserable!"

Any unpleasant emotions are willful, purposeful child insubordination. Not allowed.

The brush hangs in the air. "Wipe that snotty nose. You look like a bratty kid."

A silence. Then she hands me a kitchen towel, and I know that her mood has broken. "Let's just be CHEERFUL and get done with this, okay honey? You're making a big deal out of nothing. Be CHEERFUL! Nobody wants to see an ugly face."

She waits until I wipe my face and muster a shaky lip spread in some approximation of a smile. Thus I remain on the stool for another hour, shivering and signaling cheerfulness, head scalding into an angry, burning red, until the blessed neutralizer takes away the sting, the smell, and the interminable wait to see just what fresh hell of frizz and broken ends has been achieved this time.

Because we aren't after the natural curl of the perm, either. That uneven, chaotic mop of uncontrolled waves and kinks is an abomination and affront to Mom's beauty standards just as much as our stick-straight strands. Our hair has to manifest a perfect wave: a specific smooth, flowing bend only achieved by a daily re-torturing of our locks with hot rollers, curling irons, and overnight curlers, forcing both the natural straight and the unnatural frizz into the only form that is pleasing.

It is a thoroughly subjective and artificial beauty maintained for someone else's presumed satisfaction, painfully achieved by utterly destroying part of my body. I hate God for requiring such stupidity, and I hate my father for being somehow both complicit and absent. Even at eight I see, however impotent I am to fight it, the arbitrary nature of this denial of my natural self—how it is broken down, poisoned, forced into submission, and reconstituted into a fragile, fraying artifice in order to appeal, to please, to conform, and to live up to an expectation defined and demanded by others. Beating and pain and beauty and abject obedience to God and men are all the same, with everything entirely fake and forced. A slaughtered self, a shiny surface.

It is a lesson I learn well.

5

When I was twelve, we finally stopped moving around. Dad set up practice in the epicenter of conservative Adventism: Berrien Springs, Michigan, the one-stoplight Midwestern town where he and Mom had honeymooned decades earlier as he began his studies at the SDA seminary. Now not only could he both practice medicine and teach at the seminary, but there were multiple SDA elementary schools, an award-winning SDA secondary school, and an SDA university. It was the quintessentially isolated, rural SDA community: a dry town, no bookstores or movie theaters, no butchers, no record and poster stores, no video-rental outposts, no bowling alleys, no public swimming pools, no malls or clothing stores. Even the mail carrier and the convenience store workers were Adventist.

It was the perfect place to sequester teenaged daughters far away from worldly temptations.

To guarantee our complete protection, we lived far out of town, the same as usual—even the Adventist center was apparently deemed too rife with potential pitfalls. We always lived far enough out of range of society that people could not just drop in unannounced, which also made it extremely inconvenient (that is, mostly impossible) to have friends over or to go to other people's houses. My sister and I eventually just gave up asking to go on playdates or sleepovers; the answer was always no.

In the absence of friends, clubs, sports, television, and music, and after so many read-throughs of our pitiful book collection, I began to read the Bible itself. I had been given my own beautifully bound, gilt-edged, purse-sized edition at age eight. It had a burgundy leather cover, fragile, sheer pages, and my name stamped in gold on the front.

I began to flip through, looking eagerly for stories of women. There weren't many to choose from. Eve, whose natural curiosity destroyed humanity and introduced us to sin. Bathsheba, whose beauty was so great it inspired homicide and her own rape. Trampy man-killers: slutty Salome and traitorous Delilah, using their evil sexuality to bring about the fall of unsuspecting men. And the terrifying tales, apparently so meaningful that there needed to be two of them, of Lot offering his daughters up to a mob to be raped—which they escaped, only to later sleep with their father—and the concubine given by her husband to an entire town to rape—which she did not escape, dying in the dirt on his threshold, broken into bits and scratching at his door to be let in, after which he mailed her body parts around the country.

Then there were Rachel and Leah, with their classic mean-girl fight over the man, their dad stoking it for his own ends, tricking the hapless Jacob into marrying the ugly one first, with the final reward of marrying the pretty one years later. Barely into the double-digit age bracket, I had already internalized the logic at play, a rubric always heavily expounded in my family and clearly reinforced by the Bible: the ugly one was obviously not as worthy as the pretty one and had well-deserved problems forever after. God, not to mention her father and her husband, did not like her because she was homely. That was obviously her fault. It made perfect sense.

My favorite was always Esther, who saved her people by joining the king's harem, so beautiful and talented at whatever the harem activities were that she became the sovereign's favorite. I wanted that kind of power. Clearly, it rested mostly in looks and whatever witchery happens in harems.

Yet I knew better than to voice that ambition or to look for anything outside of what I was given, so I meekly settled in with every other kid in our church town, ready to live out the whole rest of our lives within the bumper-car track of Adventist protection, moving in monotonous little circles within the high, well-padded walls of our stifling arena, shaky Ellen White antennae extended skyward to receive that electric current from Heaven that gave meaning to our motions.

So I began to grow older.

But I didn't really get to grow up.

6

It is my fourth trip back in a week, biking several miles each way down flat country roads under dingy gray skies, a couple carrots stuffed in my back pocket to feed the horses along the way. There is only one advantage I can see to being isolated so far out of town—like we always are, no matter where we move—and I have found it: the public library.

Usually anything with the word "public" in it is dirty, dangerous, *declasse*, and denied—firmly off-limits for us: public schools, public pools, public parks, and anything else short of the Republican party. But I had been allowed to visit the library regularly once before in another Midwestern town, where I spent the summer methodically decimating the reading contest, completing each week another sheet intended to occupy the whole summer for more typical kids, whose reading time would be sandwiched between TV shows and movies and playdates and sports games and dance lessons.

I only had reading, so I piled up an obscene collection of awards—trinkets, pencils, erasers, and stickers that thrilled my soul—until I was summarily informed by the library that I was "done" in early July. It had felt like cheating; the books at my assigned reading level were so absurdly simple, something Mom reinforced with her signature scorn, calling the Berenstain Bears stupid and Dr. Seuss asinine, but I loved them anyway: the roll of language, the rhyme, the art and images, the made-up words. Unlike elsewhere in our lives, *that* kind of reading had been effortless and fun, and I had lived for checking off another title, earning another outward sign that I was good, even that I was better than others.

Achievement can be armor, but in this case it also satisfied something deep within me: the library program gave me a rare, objective measuring stick in the morass of moving goalposts and half-spoken moral expectations at home, church, and school—the ones that weighed so heavily but made so little sense. The reading contest allowed me to focus on one simple achievement: clear, well-defined rules followed by reward and recognition, all of which helped alleviate the boredom of a home devoid of music, media, and friends.

But now the library means more. I am coming for information.

Mom, as an extreme nonreader, seems not to give any thought to what lies in a public library, even such a small library as this one, tucked among Michigan farmlands. I think, to her, books are all one and the same, deadly boring and a waste of energy that could be better spent ironing the sheets or polishing the silver.

I know differently.

As a twelve-year-old I don't have to stay in the children's section anymore. I can check out more than Dr. Seuss. In this new library in this new town, I roam the entire building every weekend, eyeing each shelf, tantalizing information just waiting to be absorbed. If it is a Friday before sundown or any time on a Sunday, that one precious day per week without church or school filling nearly every waking hour, I am usually at the library.

The books themselves, however, are problematic. Anything with densely packed prose requiring more than one sitting will have to be checked out and brought home, which is infinitely dangerous. Previously I have tried squirreling away copies of paperback teen novels given to me by school friends with liberal parents, stashing these in the most unlikely places in my room or behind the locked freezer that holds the ice cream hidden from my sister, or under the footrest of the hooded-dryer beauty salon chair my grandmother backhandedly gifted my mother when she got married. But those books were always mysteriously found and disposed of, no matter how creatively I hid them. My journal, which I long to write freely in but know is not safe, also moves regularly in its space between the mattress and box spring, sometimes even managing to flip itself over. So, no. I cannot risk bringing books home until I know more about them. If just one is found to be sinful—and surely most of them are—I might lose my library privilege completely. Mom might wise up and crack down.

I check out a few "test" books—Jane Austen, Charles Dickens—but mostly I gravitate to the magazine room, its tip-tilting shelves displaying all the tantalizing issues of *Vogue* and *Cosmo*, *Teen*, and *TigerBeat* that I longingly side-eye in the grocery-store line. Juicy stacks of previous issues are available behind every cantilevered metal ledge: slide Beverly Johnson up, and there are Kim Alexis and Catherine Roberts and Isabella Rossellini and Rosemary McGrotha and Andie MacDowell, all piled one on top of the other, smoldering in bright makeup and lurid loglines. Presents! Pleasures! Diversions! Fashion Pleasers!

I return to the magazine room again and again, reading the same issues over and over. I can consume multiple issues in an hour or two before biking home. I do not yet fully realize—nor would I have cared—that these glossy fashion spreads are intended only as fleeting snapshots of style and culture, their very category, periodicals, specifying that they exist only to be outdated in a month or six and thrown into the trash.

Nothing in my world is structured that way. Every little action from birth onward is laden with life-shattering consequences; every single thing you do or say—from polishing your nails or illicitly consuming hot sauce to cheating on a test or stealing from the grocery store—even your private, unspoken thoughts—*everything* has a deadly permanence to it, a moral weight that will follow you beyond the grave.

Accordingly, I take every page in the magazines as the immutable, eternal gospel word of glamour. And what a different gospel it is! There is no dour judgment, no joyless mandate to be sober and pray unceasingly, to give up all things worldly, to serve with humility and give the glory to the Lord. No rules on dressing modestly and simply, eating sparingly of bland foods, no focus on being meek and self-effacing and pious and sexless. On the contrary, in magazine land, people do and say the most amazing things with a glee and freedom that have no repercussions. Phoebe Cates rocks straight hair, and Whitney Houston dances in a bikini in *Seventeen* magazine; Kristy McNichol and Jodie Foster brood, flirt, and make out with boys in the "movie" pages.

In Andy Warhol's new *Interview* magazine, controversial people and subject matter of all types are tossed at viewers like candy from a lurid, racy parade float. Perhaps most shockingly, flying in the face of what we are told at home—and what is implied at school—people of every race are celebrated. My sister and I have been made to understand in no uncertain terms that we, white Americans, are superior, and all others are lower. But here in magazines, there are glossy spreads glorifying Iman shimmering and Grace Jones screaming. There are fascinating profiles of Toni Morrison and Jessye Norman and Alvin Ailey and Basquiat. Their overwhelming glamor and stage presence is utterly mesmerizing to me.

And then, one day, *TIME* magazine with Brooke Shields on the cover informs me that women are actually paid for being beautiful. Paid a lot of money. For something that has been forced down my throat every day since toddlerhood, for something that was beaten into me. They are celebrated and admired for the burdensome thing that has been my very purpose for existing while remaining something I am forbidden to enjoy, call attention to, or claim credit for.

TIME's women, though, are getting all kinds of attention and credit for simply being gorgeous creatures. They are called models, and they are incredible. Apollonia—staring us down, so insolent and combative—gravity-swallowing cheekbones purple-bruised in '80s style, boobs carelessly spilling out of her shirt. Brooke, only a few years older than I, working a stunning mix of innocence and knowing, *with* her mother's encouragement! She plays the sexy pretty baby on screen but very publicly maintains a strict virginity.

I keep returning to the library throughout high school to reassure myself: yes, there *is* a world out there full of interesting people doing interesting things. Beautiful people doing beautiful things. Brilliant, rebellious, defiant people doing all those things. There is a place where people value and employ you for being pretty, that hateful thing I have endured for as long as I can remember—all those hours, all that agony soaked, pulled, and sucked into my head like the odiferous perm solutions. But it is celebrated and vaunted out there somewhere. Sometimes it is very well paid. It doesn't always have to be only for glory of God and Dad.

It could just belong to me.

I am going to find out.

But first I have to get through four years of Adventist Academy.

7

Thrilled to escape homeschooling and the embarrassingly juvenile "social studies" and "language arts" potpourri of elementary school, I was determined to get what I hoped would be a real education in high school. Even the name of the institution, Andrews Academy, sounded so classy and full of erudition. I arrived armed with a notebook full of college-rule paper and a brain starved for diversity and experience. I had secret plans to be enacted out in that glamorous magazine world, and I needed to know as much as possible. I imagined free-flowing ideas and serious intellectual discourse, researching important topics, writing papers, citing sources. I would study literature and languages! History! Maybe I would finally find out what books I needed to read at the library.

Where I dreamed of receiving a rich, varied education, however, I quickly learned there would be only more of the same as before. Sports were deemed wasteful, philosophy dangerous, film and most of the arts heathen. Evolution was forbidden, and the classics were full of idolatry, homosexuality, and critical thinking. We studied literature that eschewed most literature, the religion of only one religion, and the "science" of God's creation and the world's six-thousand-year-old natural history.

In accordance with Ellen White, instead of a broad classical education, the school's highest aim was that "students be disciplined for service . . . children must be brought to submission and obedience." On a closed, barren campus with no trees, only wide fields of grass, it was easy for our terrifyingly formal, rigidly traditional principal to crack down on potentially illicit teenage activities. We began each day with a half hour of worship in the chapel, to be followed at some point in every day's schedule with another obligatory hour of Bible or religion class—that name being a complete misnomer as the class had very little to do with religion as a broad subject and everything to do with Seventh-day Adventist doctrine. Then there were the weeks of prayer every semester, where we sat through all-day seminars on the evils of sex or preparations and rehearsals for our end-times capture, torture, and tests of faith. Outside of school hours there was youth church, chapel choir, and student ministry.

But we had lockers! The most outrageous freedom I could ever imagine: a box with a lock.

We were not allowed to choose our own locker locations since that would make it difficult for the faculty to break up "unwholesome friendships." The girl assigned to the locker next to me my sophomore year turned out to be one I knew only vaguely from the years before. Jill had been a year behind me but skipped a grade over the summer. Boyish and athletic, she had been a worthy opponent in phys-ed class in eighth grade, and I appreciated her academic ambitions having skipped a couple grades myself.

But she definitely wasn't cool. While the rest of us sported mile-high '80s hair, as much frosty eyeshadow as we were allowed, bubble bangs, and bright leg warmers and oversized sweatshirts, she swaggered around in men's flannel shirts, baggy khakis, and high tops. With a blunt, husky manner of delivery, a ragged, short haircut and stubby nails, Jill clearly did not want to be popular.

I feared this might fare badly for me socially, but halfway through the year, she disappeared without any notice or explanation. I knew I should have been more concerned, but mostly I was relieved I didn't have to stay harnessed to the uncool girl. Just as at any typical high school, being popular at Andrews Academy was *everything*.

It was hard to maintain an "in" crowd, however, without sports teams or star athletes, proms, homecomings, cheerleaders, theater stars, or dances. There was really just a simplified food pyramid of religious zeal with two basic groups: the surface believers and the "Egg Whites"—named after E. G. White, of course. There weren't many options for dissenters or mavericks, so anyone who didn't like or believe the party line gamely went along with it anyway while awaiting a chance to enter the real world. Sadly, most surface believers who escaped became some version of Egg Whites later in life, running back to the familiar after they found the real world too terrifyingly foreign and difficult to navigate.

I determined early on that I was a covert surface believer with a specialty in performance Adventism. I was bored to tears and entirely unmoved by the spiritual and religious content, but I participated enthusiastically in the chapel skits, preached during Week of Prayer, and taught a Sabbath School class. If there was a pious performance or serious sermon needed, I was there, armed with my Seal of Approval from Dad's church renown. The real Egg Whites around me, on the other hand, actually took our religion seriously. A lot of eggs were often dorky, but there were the popular and charismatic ones as well, like Cody Magnum.

Good-looking, athletic, and endowed with that racy name, Cody Magnum was a pastor-in-waiting by tenth grade, designating himself the one to save us all from the evils of rock music. He developed a soulful preaching style that he exercised at every opportunity, and teachers gave him whole class times to practice his sermonizing and play ELO backward on a boom box to dramatically expose the band's messages from the Devil.

Cody's mini-pastor efforts presaged an eventual career as the whispered leader of a splinter cult that stockpiled guns and ammunition and allegedly exhorted many of my friends' little sisters to become his virgin brides. Some combination of the church and the FBI was eventually rumored to have shut Cody down, fearing another David Koresh. It was apparently too soon after Waco to allow more bad PR to hit the press, not to mention the great embarrassment both organizations had suffered in the Branch Davidian debacle. All traces of Cody Magnum simply disappeared. He didn't resurface again for decades.

But Jill would show up again the next year.

8

"Girls, when a man goes to the store to buy a shirt, does he pick up the old, worn shirt that's wrinkled and has already been tried on? Or does he want to buy a shirt straight out of the package, all nice and folded?"

Mr. Walsh, our main religion teacher, slobbers when he speaks. Spittle gathers at the fleshy corners of his mouth like crusty snow sidelined in the wake of a snowplow. I squirm in my seat. I have not yet been kissed, but I know where this lecture is headed. The boys smirk and slink lower in their chairs.

"Of course, a man always wants a brand-new shirt!" squeals Mr. Walsh, gleefully answering his own question. "He doesn't want one that other men have handled and worn." His eyes glitter, and he shifts against the podium again while the folds of his mouth collect more foam.

We don't have sex ed here. We have obligatory "Marriage & Family" classes, in which we are regaled with all the pitfalls and sins of sex and masturbation and made to memorize charts of appropriate physical dating behavior that begins with hand-holding and, three years later, culminates in boys being so frustrated and blue-balled that who KNOWS what they might resort to. It logically has to end in marriage . . . or sin.

It is entirely the females' job to protect everyone from such a travesty. We are the temptation, the problem, so we must dedicate ourselves and our bodies to becoming the solution.

"Girls, it's up to you. Do you want to be the old, grimy shirt left on the floor of the dressing room, tried on and trampled by anyone who comes in? Wrinkled and soiled and stretched out? Or do you want to be purchased fresh in the package?"

I briefly, if strangely, picture what kind of shirt I would be: the traditional kind like my father wears, of course, with French cuffs and a pointed collar. Jewelry is forbidden for Adventists, but cufflinks live in a gray area, like brooches and hiking on Saturdays. I would absolutely require elaborate cufflinks and definitely be 100% cotton. My mother always complains bitterly about my father's 100% cotton shirts—they require too much care, and she refuses to indulge that—but I love to iron them. The soft cotton, so smooth and silky out of the dryer, becomes stiff and formal under the brutal heat of the steaming iron, a process nearly identical to the correction of my ugly hair. Someone would definitely have to overheat and starch me. It seems fitting.

A look from Mr. Walsh jolts me back to the issue at hand: Do I want to be an old, used shirt, tried on by many men? Or do I want to remain properly packaged and suffocated in cellophane: folded, neatly on display, arms contorted in excruciating origami shapes behind my back, so immobilized with pins that I stab the unsuspecting wearer?

I steal a glance at Carol Christensen, a timid, fuzzy-sweatered girl with oddly domed 1950s hausfrau hair and a mincing walk. Everyone else often stares too, including Mr. Walsh. We know that Carol has a serious boyfriend, a *non-Adventist* boyfriend, and that Mr. Walsh has been devoting long, mysterious hours behind his closed office door to counseling her privately about the risks to her purity. If anyone is headed for the Goodwill shirt bin, it is understood to be Carol.

Mr. Walsh begins to read from one of his favorite Adventist texts, *On Becoming a Woman*. There is supposedly a matching book for boys, but none of us have seen it or even know the name. Apparently their becoming isn't as important as our becoming.

"A young woman carries a personal responsibility to avoid

conversations, gestures, and dress that would arouse physical attraction. A Christian girl . . ." Mr. Walsh pauses for effect and to daub ineffectually at the gathering spittle. "A Christian girl will learn to resist such familiarities by young men in such a *gracious* way as not to create offense."

Say no without appearing to say no. Always be pleasing, never create offense. Obey, but don't submit. No, always submit, but don't sin. Don't say no, but don't seduce. Be attractive, but don't attract. It's all your responsibility, but don't you dare try to find out what it all actually is.

As he drones on, I stare at the cover of the book in his hands. It is painted in lurid, pulp-fiction Technicolor: A dark-haired girl in a Peter Pan collar poses stiffly in the foreground, her sad gaze going right through us. Two young men lounge in the background, leering at her with clean-cut, preppy predation. The artist is surely trying for a girl who is "pure and demure," but what he achieved was "terrified but resigned."

I look across the room at Jill, who showed up again at the beginning of the semester as quietly as she had disappeared. But this is a very changed Jill. Bone-thin and nervous, all of her swagger and sporty muscle gone, she wears every day to school the lace-bibbed floral dresses with poufy sleeves that most of us save for church. Her hair is now teased and sprayed and curled like the rest of ours. She sits—cowers, really—beside her brooding, silent boyfriend, a guy two years her elder whom everyone agrees is weird and antisocial, their desks nearly touching.

This entire class is structured to tell us how dangerous and off-limits dating is, and yet the school is throwing Jill in Ben's lap.

Rumor has it she had a nervous breakdown. Rumor has it she tried to commit suicide. Rumor has it she was sent to California for some mysterious operation for some mysterious sexual aberration. Rumor has it she was shipped off to a "conversion camp." That one really confuses me, because she is already Adventist;

why did she need to be converted?

Nobody knows for sure, and Jill isn't saying. In fact, she never talks at all anymore.

I look away and take out pen and paper. The girls are writing essays on staying as pure as untouched linen until marriage. My face burns as the boys look on, snickering. The classroom grows quiet as our female half bends over the faux laundry assignment on our desks. Mr. Walsh licks his lips audibly. Sam MacDonough flicks paperclips at the ceiling. I can feel Larry Canard reading over my shoulder, breathing down my neck. He snorts gleefully.

I watch Jill, glued glumly to Ben's side.

I watch Mr. Walsh, now with a strange horror. He is breathing shallowly, literally rubbing against the podium, shifting behind it and staring fixedly at Carol Christensen.

Somehow this is all wrong. I refuse to write another word.

But.

If I don't comply—if I do anything but exactly what I'm told to do—will I also then have to attend private, one-on-one meetings in his office?

Will I be sent away somewhere like Jill, for something that I don't understand, that will change me forever?

The rules and standards are never clear, but one thing is: this is all clearly our fault, our responsibility. Us girls.

I look at Carol. I look at Jill.

I take up my pen, and I write.

9

That day I write a critical paper on my favorite Bible character, Esther, and the uncle who prostituted her to the king's harem in order to save her people. I am proud of my scholarship and thrilled at my attempt at critical thinking. My thesis question asks, "Does the end justify the means?"

No sooner has my paper hit the teacher's desk than I am called into a days-long process of concerned conferences, prayer sessions, parent-teacher consultations, and a stern reprimand session from the principal. I can't really be punished because I have done nothing overtly wrong, but I am wrong anyway and require strict controlling and correction. My questioning the rules equals doubt, and doubt is a sin. Critical thinking is a road to letting the Devil in, particularly when a girl suggests harlotry can be useful.

I was immediately, insistently drowned in the pious advice of Ellen White, over and over: "Distrust your own judgment, and depend on the judgment of God. Do God's will submissively . . . following your own way and your own will, you will find thorns and thistles, and you will lose the reward." Whenever I would try to argue that I was just saying what happened in the Bible, I was hit with more Ellen White: "It is a sin to doubt. The least unbelief, if cherished, involves the soul in guilt, and brings great darkness and discouragement."

My father was so devoted to reading and rereading her every scribble, and all of my teachers seemed sure that her guidance would save me, that I did try to resign myself to her counsel. I wanted to do what my community wanted—but there was so little to celebrate and so much to condemn. There was not a single thing or thought that White did not scorn; even my beloved magazines came under her prohibition: "Do not fill the house with magazines . . . the Lord has nothing to do with such reading. It fills the mind with trash . . . It is a sin in the sight of God to give the mind to such reading . . . We have no time to spend in light reading." The more I tried to obediently absorb and follow her direction, the more I began to hate our grim, joyless, busybody prophet. She peered into everyone's lives from the grave, pompously and in nauseating detail correcting, controlling, and commanding until we gave up every pleasure and interest.

Eventually my subjection to the earnest, self-righteous deprogramming meetings ended when my mother, a college classmate of our terrifying principal, stormed into his office and told him there would be no more. This was just one of many twists and turns in my complicated relationship with my mother, fraught as it was with setbacks and little self-reflection on her part yet sustained by her fierce and unceasing defense of her children. I was extremely grateful to her, not to mention very admiring, in that moment.

But that moment also brought a sudden realization of how terrified all of the adults were. Why had they come down so hard on me, and what was everyone so scared of? I knew they were afraid we would somehow lose our salvation; that seemed honest enough. But there was something else going on, too. Could salvation alone account for needing to control our every thought and breath and act?

That subterranean panic must indicate we were being deprived of something exciting and powerful. The Esther Experiment confirmed two things for me: First, that I did not believe in the Seventh-day Adventist Church or its doctrines, or even basic Christian teachings, and I wasn't sure if I ever had. It also touched a raw nerve at the heart of both Adventism and my own family, and this had something to do with the details of Esther's particular story. So many of her circumstances were intimately familiar to me: be pretty and accommodating; do as you're told; pleasing men is your highest calling. But in that now familiar self-contradiction, something that she did was right but wrong, and we were to celebrate how it worked for God but not to question or emulate it.

I didn't know quite what that something was, but I suspected Esther did more to be pleasing to the king than curling her hair and staying cheerful, and I was going to find out. I just had to bide my time until I could escape.

For now, however, I had only gained a miserable new insight into how necessary it was to remain compliant at all costs. How much safer to stay silent, not make any waves, submit, obey, and never, ever, ever question the men in authority.

10

At 7 p.m. I lie quietly in my bed, listening to my father's heavy footfalls coming down the hallway. His feet are extra wide, so his shoes are specially made: stiff, black leather wingtips with heavy stacked leather soles. They are magnificent, and I adore their old-fashioned formality. The uppers last for years, although the soles need redoing every so often because Dad paces in circles to think or practice sermons, gesturing and muttering to himself, until the soles develop whorled smooth spots, eventually reaching a paper-thin consistency under the balls of his feet.

Dad isn't pacing in circles now, though. He is hunting.

I lie very still in my bed, practicing long, slow, deep breaths. It is quite early in the evening, but I am asleep. I am asleep. I try to keep my eyelids still; squeezing them tight is for amateurs. I am after the smoothly relaxed lids of true slumber.

Relax. *Relax.*

When we moved to Michigan, my mother let my sister and I each choose our own room décor. Giddy with this rare liberty, and always seeking the glamorous life, I demanded an enormous, glitzy wallpaper mural of a tropical beach scene, for which Mom painstakingly handstitched a gorgeous matching seashell-covered duvet. My sister, by contrast, meekly took whatever was offered and ended up with a floral and chintz display worthy of an upscale retirement home in her room across the hall.

Dad's footsteps pause just outside the door; has he come for me or her? My reflexes nearly give me away as I tense beneath my seashells, but I manage to avoid creaking the bedframe. Then my stomach rumbles, and the room echoes with unruly gastric commentary. I skipped dinner again, and the sourdough biscuit I had for lunch is long gone. Does the belly gurgle if you are truly asleep? I fear intestinal betrayal.

The doorknob rattles ominously, and I can hear Dad mumble something low, his deep voice cracking awkwardly as he strains for lightness and humor. He is talking to my sister; she must have been caught in the hallway. I try again for still, somnolent bliss. *Please God, please just make him go away.*

Through squinted lids I can see the knob on my unlockable door turn as if possessed by the Devil, just like in the missionary stories that terrified me as a child. I wish again for a lock. I hold my breath. *Maybe he will just look in and go away.*

"Miss?" His voice has the singsong, sickly sweet tone it always has at this time of night, so unbecoming for a naturally booming orator's voice. I loathe the falsetto and the falsehood, bewildered by the odd compulsion that turns my charming, intellectual hero into a syrupy bully. If there was anything in my stomach besides the memory of a sourdough biscuit, I would be heaving. Instead, I clutch my cotton shells tightly and hold totally still.

The heavy tread of stiff, resoled wingtips comes closer. I dare not breathe. *No, wrong!* I have to breathe long, deep, easy breaths. *Breathe, Melissa, breathe. You are sleeping. You are asleep.*

He stops a foot away from the bed.

"Miss?" Again, the chipper car salesman tone. "It's time for wort-chip!"

Every night we gather in the living room for family worship to read aloud passages from the Bible or from books by Ellen White. At the moment, we are deep into one of the hefty tomes in her *Conflict of the Ages* series. I have paid so little attention, I'm not sure which one, but it suddenly seems important. I mentally recite the titles to slow my breathing: *Acts of the Apostles, The Great Controversy, Desire of Ages* . . . there, is that it? It's a dismal book, despite the racy, drugstore romance title, a dull and endlessly detailed tale of God throwing the Devil out of Heaven. Or was it the book in which she warned us ominously of the end-times terrors and tortures we—the one true remnant church—would be put through by Satan and his followers? It had all been given to Ellen White in various visions and trances. At one point, she stood holding a heavy Bible aloft in one hand for an entire day, staring at the ceiling and reciting the history of the Devil's downfall as God revealed it to her. Some might say she was possessed, like in those missionary stories of pagan tribes and their demons that still scare the bejeesus out of me at this age. But *her* version of spirituality, I've been given to understand, was somehow divinely inspired, by the only correct divine.

"Wort-chip time!" Dad sings out once more, gaily, with the same cutesy mispronunciation, like a kindergarten teacher announcing cookies and milk. Of course, I wouldn't really know what that's like, would I, having been homeschooled during those formative years and generally forbidden sugary treats.

I can't tell if it's the idea of contraband cookies on an empty stomach, the prospect of revisiting the same theological themes for the hundredth time, or having my brilliant, suave father trilling the evening's designated activity in bright, bubbly baby talk—but some combination of it all makes the bile crawl up the back of my throat. It burns on the raw patches dug by my fingernails during the half dozen times today that I purged.

Breathe. Breathe.

There is never another excuse to skip worship. Homework, intramural games, friends visiting, sickness—nothing. The only thing that works is sleep. With school days consumed by daily enforced chapel attendance and Adventist doctrine classes and Saturdays devoted solely to church and other religious activities—no choice whatsoever allowed in the grinding repetition—my theological breadbasket is stuffed to overflowing.

So, this year I began to arrange my schedule to be in bed by 6 p.m., feigning sleep in order to avoid the final, hateful coercion of the day. I can circumvent both family dinner and worship this way, simultaneously controlling my corporeal intake and scriptural force-feeding. Since I can find peace and quiet only in the wee hours of the morning, I have begun to get up at 2 a.m. to do my homework, lying on the floor in my bathroom.

My ribs get sore from stretching out prone to pore over assignments for long stints in the wee hours, but as my only arena of semiautonomy, it is pure luxury: no one is ever awake to micromanage me, and the door is as good as locked. The heating vent runs along the floorboards—a cozy situation during frigid Michigan winters—not to mention the bathroom houses my two sets of hot rollers and curling irons that begin their several hours' service at dawn.

This domestic swing shift of mine works only some of the time, however. Right now I lie frozen, feeling the tension in the room. *Dad is onto me, isn't he?* He is a doctor, after all; they probably have a visual checklist of bodily indicators for everything: dead, asleep, awake, comatose. *Am I mistakenly playing dead?*

I cannot breathe. *Are my eyelids relaxed enough?* I feel him hovering over my possum pose. He must be debating whether to call my bluff.

There is a long pause. I wonder what he is looking at, what he is waiting for. At length, I hear his custom-fit footsteps recede. The door closes softly, and the heavy tread resumes. His voice across the hall is muffled now by the unlockable door between us.

"Soph?" He hails my sister heartily. "Time for wort-chip!"

11

Even though I was able to mostly tune out the forced Ellen White readings at school, she was omnipresent at home. Her pedantic guidance invaded every corner since, according to her, nothing about our life was our own: "Children are to be instructed that they are the Lord's property, bought with His own precious blood, and that they cannot live a life of pleasure and vanity, have their own will and carry out their own ideas . . ." Creepy, paralyzing, crazy guilt-inducing, this teaching rang false in my gut—but my gut was from the Devil, right? Ellen said that too.

As a result, since we were denied any autonomy whatsoever, day or night, at school or at home, Sophia and I each turned inward in a desperate attempt to exert some sort of control over at least one thing in our lives: our bodies. Independently of one another, we both began to self-harm, each thinking we were all alone in that dark, forbidden behavior. One of the easiest ways to stake a claim to self-management was with our food intake. They could force us into below-the-knee skirts, curled hair, and one-piece bathing suits, and they could even restrict our diet to the vegetarian, flavorless, Egg White decrees, but they could not control how much we ate.

My sister doubled down on hoarding and consuming junk food, stockpiling candy bars and stealing Little Debbies—the Adventist-sanctioned, lard-less snack—from the local drugstore and consuming them in secret binges. It was something she had done since she was a young child, but it only became a problem when she went through puberty and the pressure to be physically pleasing and attractive intensified severely. My parents set in on years of torture: shaming her in front of the family, sending her to our vain and rigid grandmother for summers of "weight loss camp," bribing her with money, gym memberships, and new clothes, and forcing her on liquid diets. My mother would buy fancy new clothes for Soph—in one instance, an expensive new ski suit, several sizes too small—and hang them in her room, on display, as motivation. When my sister failed to lose the weight, the item would be ostentatiously returned with great disgust, and Sophia would be forced to wear her old, too-tight suit for the entire winter as punishment for her failure.

Sophia had always been extremely athletic, drop-dead gorgeous, and never at any time anywhere near obese or unhealthy, but that didn't matter. There was an ideal she needed to achieve according to enigmatic family appearance metrics, and when none of my parents' (and other assorted relatives') efforts resulted in a thinness that they found acceptable, they withdrew her from her first year of college. She would not be allowed to return until she lost the required poundage. They were holding her education hostage until she conformed to their body-image desires.

Our looks were far more important than our brains and schooling. My terror at this realization hit a whole new level as I watched Sophia; being deprived of a chance at education was the worst thing I could imagine. I immediately began to assert obsessive control over my food intake, sliding firmly into a decades-long battle with anorexia and bulimia. I skipped breakfast and took tiny baggies of air-popped popcorn and carrots for lunch. Snacks were never even a consideration since Ellen White had declared them an abomination, so most days I fueled an eight-to-ten-hour school day—which always included PE and usually an afternoon intramurals game or practice—with a bag of oil-less popcorn and raw vegetables.

Mom knew full well how little I was consuming—nothing about our bodies and looks escaped her notice, from the need to iron a skirt to the amount of blush on our cheeks—but she did not discourage me. My physician father warned me only against eating too many carrots: they would turn me an unattractive orange color.

I took up long-distance running and working out to Jane Fonda's aerobics record after school, on top of the exercise I was already getting. After days of the virtual starvation I would give in and buy loads of treats at the gas station on the way home from school, inhaling them quickly and pulling over to make myself throw up before I got home. Soon I was bingeing and purging daily. I began running my fingers obsessively through my hair, pulling it out bit by bit. I chewed my cuticles into bloody divots and ripped the skin off my lips until there were constant scabs under my school-inspection-approved light pink lipstick.

I absolutely refused to suffer the same fate as my sister. Come hell or high water, I would be good. I would be so skinny they would never withhold college from me.

It was my only way out.

I would be the best. I would be absolutely perfect.

12

"I throw up every day, Mom!" I scream. "I have thrown up every day of high school so far, and then I went away for the summer—and it stopped!"

My mother blinks.

"I'm bulimic, Mom! And it's because of YOU. It's because of . . . ALL THIS! When I come home, it starts, and when I get away, it magically disappears!"

I can hear my sister pad quietly out of the adjacent living room. She hates confrontation more than anyone I know.

I took myself away for the summer to visit distant relatives who were marginally (i.e. definitely not) Adventist. It was a trip not terribly approved by my parents, but they had not been able to stop me because I had secretly arranged and paid for it all with cash from my summer job and selling vintage clothes I had picked up at thrift stores. I had not told anyone about the trip until I was almost ready to leave and Mom had eavesdropped on one of my secret planning phone calls. By then it was too late; my trip was booked, the relatives had said yes, and a friend was waiting to take me to the airport.

To my surprise, my self-destructive habits dramatically dropped from a boil to barely a simmer as soon as I left.

"Oh, honey . . ." My mother flails. She floats unsteadily toward a chair and collapses, her torso continuing in motion a few seconds after she sits before deflating slowly, like the hot-air balloons we would watch land in the valley sometimes below my dad's family ranch in Napa.

I stand and wait. We are in entirely new territory: I have said something honest. Something unpleasant.

"Oh, honey," she says again. I have never seen my mother at a loss for words. She finally begins, tenuously, reaching, struggling. "You have a problem, obviously. I . . . I don't know anything about these things. We didn't have eating disorders when I was growing up. If there's something wrong with you, we need to figure it out. What can we do?"

Suddenly giddy with emotional release, I feel a rush of love for her. We are going to have a new relationship from now on, my mother and I—*I can actually be honest with her and she will listen!* I don't have to always secretly plan and execute my desires—I might be able to express my wishes and have them honored! My needs will be acknowledged and met!

"I don't know, Mom. It was like I was magically cured when I wasn't here. I just can't live here. You're too . . . you're . . ." I lean against the doorway for support, reality catching up to me. There is a limit to how openly I can speak. We are new at this. "There's just . . . there's something about being here that makes me bulimic."

The dining room fills with silence for a moment. Then my mother's words burst forth in their customary torrent, issuing marching orders to her vertebrae, which restack into their usual erect, military posture.

"I have an idea, honey! Would you like to go see a therapist?" She brightens and bounces out of her chair. "A counselor of some kind, maybe? Ginny Slater knows a lot of good Adventist counselors, I can call her right now and ask for a recommendation. Why don't we do that, honey?" She smiles indulgently. "Then you can get away from me and the house and talk to someone and it will be confidential, and maybe they can help you with this. You can't go on like that, honey. It's not healthy."

That was too easy, and it's all wrong and going too fast: "Adventist" and "Confidential" cancel each other out in my world.

Now the smile is gone, replaced by a familiar, tight look of disapproval and remonstrance: "*You* have a problem, honey—you are not well, and I can't help you with that. We need to find a way to take care of it and make you right again. An Adventist therapist will know just how to help you." She rushes past me to the phone and begins dialing.

I go up to my room and wedge a shoe against the door. There are still no locks on our doors even though I am nearly eighteen, but since I am messy, I normally get away with placing a pile of clothing against the door to appear accidental while providing a few seconds' insulation against swooping maternal recon missions. Today, however, merits a full-on shoe blockade, inquisitions be damned.

In my dressing room—part of a suite of rooms I have claimed in the rambling Victorian fixer-upper that is our current "way out of town" home—I pull down a box marked "BOOKS" in enormous black letters and remove the top layer of biographies. Mom detests books, never missing a chance to make bitter jabs at Dad's lavish, well-loved library. I have given this some thought and decided that biographies are at the very bottom of her list: why read about other people's lives when you think everyone is immoral and "the world" is a scary, evil place?

Safely stashed beneath Beryl Markham's autobiography of high-flying feminist adventures in the African bush is a stack of Little Debbie snack cakes. Although the southern Adventist family who owns the company is viewed with slightly sneering suspicion because they have gotten rich and gone mainstream with their product, their treats are still considered the only morally acceptable indulgence because they have never contained lard.

Next to the piles of gooey Oatmeal Pies, flaky Nutty Bars, and Swiss Rolls is a neat trio of Slimfast chocolate shakes. Mom and Dad are currently enforcing a Slimfast diet for Sophia. She's not allowed to eat anything outside of their purview, especially not such decadent sweets. She is not allowed to go back to college until she loses thirty pounds on the chalky sludge meal replacement system. I carefully steal one shake every time they bring home her nutritional allotment and secret it under Beryl.

With one eye on my phone—the "busy" light is on, indicating Mom is still on the extension downstairs—I carefully line up six oatmeal pies and six chocolate cupcakes, removing each plastic covering with one practiced rip. Working quickly, I stuff the telltale wrappers in my bra for later flushing down the toilet, one by one, torn in pieces. They are prickly and uncomfortable, crackling like baby diapers against my sweating skin.

I pop open the can of Slimfast and toss my head back, gulping down the slimy mixture in three fast swallows while skipping as much of the dusty taste as possible.

Thick liquids are a key preparatory stomach coating for a good binge and purge.

13

After three mostly useless counseling sessions with the Adventist therapist, things went right back to normal, or possibly worse. As my upperclassman years dwindled leading up to my final run for the exits, my mother became wildly more controlling, exercising a suffocating vigilance. At that point there was no use in fighting back any longer. I just had to endure and keep my eye on the prize: escape.

She stopped at nothing to extract our submission in all things, and now that I had seen getting away *did* make things better, my trapped feeling was excruciating. I continued half-hearted attempts to rebel for as long as I could, but as the problem child, the "strong-willed child" (per James Dobson), I was the one whose will had to be broken with whatever worked. Physical beatings had been not infrequent ever since I was tiny, from pinches, digs, and slaps to welts from a leather belt, paddle hairbrushes, and, in one epic battle, my mother's college cello bow, which she broke across my back.

Not only did Dobson—the evangelical Christian's go-to Dr. Spock alternative—highly encourage beating children to break their will, but Egg White was, of course, all-in too . . . but only when the whipping was done with *love*: "Whipping may be necessary . . . the child should be seriously impressed with the thought that this is for the child's own good. He should be taught that every fault uncorrected will bring unhappiness to himself . . . children will find their greatest happiness in submitting their wills . . ." Thus the belt, the hairbrush, and the cello bow came with some half-defined, grim, shameful pretense at love along with a command to submit, forgive, and understand that it was all my fault. There was an odd mix of parental shame and superiority, as if they somehow knew what they were doing was wrong, but they were earning gold stars by doing it. It had always been enormously confusing and humiliating, but even the idea of that old mix of pain and love and submission and shame seemed now somehow dirty and deeply wrong, so I gave up trying to assert myself in any manner.

Sophia, three years older than I and with a distinctly softer personality, had always been mortified by my raging fights and voluntarily, furtively broke her own will somewhere along the line, devoting herself to being forever pliable and mostly invisible, never expressing an opinion or a need. Eventually she went away to Adventist college and began to timidly explore her own freedom, but when at home she, like me, fell back into her own soothing self-destruction: comforting herself more and more with stolen food and late-night bingefests and attempts at an artistic career which my parents refused to acknowledge as "serious." It was an open secret that our bedrooms were frequently searched for contraband clothing, teen magazines, novels, and pop music. Sophia's was also searched for food. Our personal mail and diaries were read. Phone calls with friends almost always contained moments of muffled clicks when the extension line was picked up or stealthily returned to the cradle, the telltale noise created by a thumb letting go of the switch hook an instant before the handset makes contact with the base.

Mom continued to micromanage our bodies, still parroting my grandmother's bizarrely coercive words: "Your father likes it when you look pretty." She had eventually given up the battles over perms, but we were otherwise still held to the same beauty standard as always with undisguised disgust, shaming, and refusals to let us leave the house if our appearances were not perfectly to her liking. Terrified of any hint of sexuality, yet insisting that we be thin and beautiful ostensibly to please and keep the men we were not yet allowed to date, Mom controlled everything as we neared the end of our Academy careers: we were not allowed to go without makeup ("You look like an old washerwoman!"), but we were not allowed to wear too much ("You look like a floozy!"), and we always had to "Stand up straight!" because slumping, in Mom's eyes, was ugly, slovenly, and somehow associated with sluttiness.

Nobody at school could tell that we were so completely micromanaged, though, because I was hot on that college track. A good student, a model student. The best. I made the Honor Society, I earned badges and awards in sports, academics, extra-curriculars, and the all-important religious service. I was an enthusiastic participant in all school functions, a regular on the platform for morning chapel, a dependable member of every volunteer squad, a squeaky-clean mentor to younger students, industriously building that all-important resume for university applications. Perfection, pleasing, and presentation were working well for me. I had become a master at parroting, pretending, and performing up to others' expectations. I was so close to getting out. I couldn't stop now.

I was good at being good. Very, very good.

But it was getting harder.

14

I would only know all of that much later, of course, after years of deconstruction and therapy showed me the multiple layers of dysfunction, disembodiment, and dysregulation I was channeling every Sabbath. But no, *this* Sabbath was one of those rare chances for me to share the dramatic spotlight, if only by family association. Preparing to saunter up the church aisle, I carefully hold my folded coat out on my arm in order to display the slim silhouette of my mother's green velvet cocktail dress. She is much shorter, and I only rarely fit into her wasp-waisted, skintight 1950s sheath, even after endless bouts of throwing up carrot sticks and popcorn, so I am not going to blow this presentation.

The front of the church presents two large, sturdy wooden pulpits that jut out on either side of the stage like the prows of small ships (sadly bereft of any lascivious, half-naked figureheads), though they are now rendered forlorn and obsolete by an incongruous '80s plexiglass speaker's stand in center stage, which was introduced with great fanfare to bring "a transparent connection" between the preacher and his flock. The comfortably padded pews—hundreds deep and four abreast—are divided by wide aisles down which we teenagers parade before the service, scoping each other out while pretending to look for our parents like a prim, religious *American Graffiti*. I am upping that drama for my own amusement, hoping to catch the eye of an older guy I've had a crush on by attempting the stroll quite late, right before opening prayer. Church is already technically in session, and I am entering right beside the pulpits, heading straight down the aisle and directly into the face of thousands of worshippers. All these people can either watch me as I walk in or old Deacon Marcone as he coughs and directs them in a listless monotone to the final bulletin announcements.

It is risky to walk in from the front of the church, but with my father scheduled to preach, I am full of confidence and superiority. Dad doesn't preach often, and his sermons are greatly anticipated because they deliver the closest thing to drama and theater that our dull, sober community has. Today I am determined to claim some cast-off limelight and be part of the dramatic prelude, if just for a moment.

Other preachers are plebian, doling out trite spiritual comfort for the "hoi polloi" (a Greek word Dad taught me that I love to toss about). They read a passage from the Bible as if they are the only ones to have ever stumbled upon it, awkwardly relate it to everyday life, expound on a one-note theme, and then call everyone to Christ. Or they harangue us with warnings of the Sunday Law and our coming persecution. In brilliant contrast, my father's sermons are full of tension and history, details and stories. Biblical figures come alive in full Technicolor, storming about, doing fearsome things, warts and all, with an intriguing dash of ancient languages, archaeology, and geography.

Everyone is always slightly in awe of Dad: he is revered for the many hats he wears as a medical doctor, biblical scholar, missionary, seminarian, and orator. With a booming voice, a kind of impish, self-deprecating humor, and meticulous scholarship, he preaches, teaches, ministers, and heals. He's the closest thing to a saint that Adventists have. His medical missionary trips to Africa, Asia, and Eastern Europe add to his aura of power and mystique. I am stalking through the Pioneer Memorial Church in a halo of glory-by-association, and I love every minute of it.

Adventists do not have megachurches (that would be tacky and misdirect the glory from God to man), but Pioneer comes close; it is the home church of the Adventist seminary and the associated university. The sanctuary of the huge, gray stone monstrosity is purposely dull and unornamented inside and out so as to broadcast loudly, "We're not like those *Catholics*!" No scenes of Christ's life or crucifixes adorn the walls and certainly no gilt or other distracting elements that might encourage idolatry; the stained-glass windows boast only abstract shapes, the ledges and podiums hold only flowers.

I have already spied where Mom is sitting. She considers herself too free-spirited to have a "regular spot" like most of the other prominent families, so we have to hunt for her every week (but never in the balcony—that is the sole domain of delinquent teenagers and visitors who don't know anybody). I begin to saunter toward her: head up, coat out, stomach in, don't look down, don't look down. Only those who can't handle the scrutiny look at the floor. I finally reach the pew and slide in next to my sister.

I spend the opening hymn, comments, and prayers counting the number of vowels and consonants in the program. Then I count how many times the earnest old deacon says "Lord" while he prays. I remove the little rubber liners from the hymnal rack that are intended to hold empty glasses after the grape juice is drunk (not wine! We're not like those Catholics!) at the quarterly Communion. Using them as stencils, I draw round-eyed, round-breasted, round-hipped women on the tithe envelopes, then tuck them back into the rack for some scandalized tithe-payer to pray over later.

Finally, it is Dad's turn to speak. I put away my doodling and compose myself in a Nancy Reagan gaze of adoration. Dad proceeds with measured steps from the pew on the side of the platform to the center stage. When he steps behind the plexiglass podium, I am momentarily embarrassed, like I am for every preacher every week, as his upper and lower halves are bisected by the see-through pulpit shelf. We now view Dad from the waist down at a watery remove, his legs and hips distorted as though he were standing in a fish tank.

I am greatly annoyed that this destroys my enjoyment of his renowned ritual: he methodically opens his Bible, places it on the pulpit, and steps back again. The church falls into a grand hush. Even the lone cougher who interrupts every official silence manages to stifle the phlegm momentarily. My father folds his hands, bows his head, and prays.

Not out loud. Not for us. He just stands silently before the entire church and takes a moment of numinous communion with his God. No one else ever does this; it's my dad's thing.

I thrill to the intense spectacle of it all. Finally, he finishes his silent prayer and steps forward to grasp the sides of the clear plastic lectern. I try to ignore the lower half of his body moving just a millisecond behind the upper half, delayed by the plexiglass viewing column. Deep, loud, and strong, with a dusky, cracking cadence, my father begins to speak. I swell with pride.

"It is the first day of spring, but there is no celebrating in Mesopotamia," he begins. "As the sun rises on one of the most fearsome cities in the world, its enormous gates swing slowly open. Two gates to the east, two gates to the west. From the most fearsome city pours out the most fearsome force, eight abreast, in equal columns proceeding east and west. The Assyrian army is campaigning again, and they will not return until the first day of winter."

I smile and settle in. I will possibly need to remember the Assyrians tomorrow for my secret SATs.

15

Adventist high schools at the time refused to administer SATs because their colleges only used the ACT for admissions. SATs, of course, were the only accepted admissions test for nearly every other competitive, non-Adventist (i.e., real) university. I secretly researched everything I could about these gold-standard, get-in-so-you-can-get-out exams I would need to ace. They were only administered on Saturdays, and only at the public high schools in our township, unless specially requested and arranged differently. That worked out really well for everyone who wanted to keep myself and my peers in the Adventist tumbler. Our guidance counselors would only talk to us about Adventist higher education opportunities, presenting us with only one option: take the ACT and go to the Adventist college of your choice. But they hadn't reckoned on my knowledge of the public library.

From my first days as a freshman I had spent many furtive Sunday afternoons there reading university catalogs, eyes widening at the incredible number and diversity of classes. I read each description, scrutinized every campus, and memorized all their admissions standards. My research warned me it was a difficult process to request and arrange a special SAT, particularly on a day other than Saturday. The requests had to be made in writing, a school-certified proctor had to be available to administer and monitor the test, and it had to be taken under approved conditions.

Somehow, two other juniors and I—even though we were all from different social groups —found each other secretly and figured out how to arrange a special SAT on a Sunday. No matter how hard I try, I don't remember how or where we did it. I only remember the paralyzing fear—the fear of getting caught, the terror of doing something bad. The shame and sin of simply wanting to go to a good school created a fear so intense that I have blocked the details out to this day—all the details except for one, which remains crystal clear after all these years: archipelago. I missed only one question on the verbal section, failing perfection by that one word.

Of the three of us sequestered away in a small room I can't picture somewhere with a proctor I can't remember, one, a boy, ended up a hard-boiled Egg—a brilliant biblical archaeologist and SDA university professor. But the other two of us, both girls, went on to Ivy League colleges and made it all the way out, forever. And one of those two—the one I wasn't—went brilliantly further to collect multiple graduate degrees from other distinguished universities, to work for NASA, to become a renowned professor, and to make history as part of the team that created and launched the Mars Explorer.

With SATs checked off my list and Ivy League applications lined up, I turned my future ambitions to mastering everything that was forbidden. I knew better than to start experimenting with anything while still nestled in the bosom of Adventism, so, not sure how far afield was safe, I aimed for blackout conditions as far away as possible.

Back at the public library once again, I discovered through compulsively reading the newspaper that the son of my late hero Bobby Kennedy was running for office in Boston. With equal parts desperation and naive ambition I decided I was going to do my experimenting on the doorstep of a famous family halfway across the country. I somehow convinced my parents to let me apply for an internship on Joe Kennedy Jr.'s first congressional campaign. We jointly convinced my principal to let me off the school tour bus on a rainy corner in Boston during our junior-year "Constitutional

United States" trip so that I could interview. Astonishingly, I later realized the campaign didn't actually have any official internships, but they granted me an interview anyway. The whole thing convinced Kennedy Jr.'s campaign manager to create an internship in the finance department just for me.

If that wasn't dumbfounding enough, my parents let me go. They were staunch Republicans, as was my school principal, but the glamour and sheer novelty of it all was simply too much, I think, for everyone, even if Kennedy was a Democrat. My mother put aside her thorough disgust and fear of life outside SDA boundaries and doggedly set out to live with me in an Adventist college dorm more than an hour outside of Boston so that I could pursue my dream. She was grim but supportive.

At the time, I couldn't have told you what Joe's platform was, what he believed in, or what I believed. I had no idea what I would be doing or what to expect, and I really didn't care. I was there to finally see what the real world was like and rub elbows with famous people, especially those of this family I had worshipped since first discovering their mystique in old *LIFE* magazines.

At first the glamor was sparse; I spent every weekday for six weeks driving an hour and a half to Boston in my little Honda Civic, doing menial tasks, cold-calling potential donors, and then driving the hour and a half back to the dorm. I didn't know anybody, and I was younger than everyone else. Mostly I tried to sell fundraiser tickets over the phone—a loathsome task, but one I undertook with grim dedication in order to justify my presence in that space. It really didn't matter to me what I did. I was simply thrilled that my dream was coming along.

It was so intoxicating. I was inching closer and closer to finding out all the things everyone had been hiding from me my whole life, and I was doing it in the center of more star power than I had ever dreamed. I met most of the young Kennedy cousins, including my longtime crush JFK Jr. (more impossibly good-looking in real life than any magazine picture ever conveyed), and was thrilled to be stationed mere steps from the office of my department head—Michael Kennedy—who left me quite speechless with his striking resemblance to his famous father.

Occasionally Michael would ask me, though I had less than a years' experience behind the wheel, to drive him across town to RFK Jr's Waterkeeper Alliance offices. Upon discovering that I would follow orders without question, he gleefully directed me to swerve across multiple lanes, then to switch back in a panic. The famous Kennedy recklessness and laughter were infectious, and I looked forward to our wild drives across town even when I was petrified that the next one would be my last moments on earth.

Near the end of my two months at the campaign, I discovered to my delight that Rory—Bobby's youngest child, Joe and Michael's baby sister, and exactly my age—was working in the campaign room around the corner from me. Here was my chance to make my first real-world friend.

Screwing up my courage, I venture from my designated fundraising room into the heart of campaign headquarters. What is called "the war room" is embedded off the back corner of the cavernous general space across from Joe's office. His omnipresent assistant hovers in and out, and Joe occasionally pops out himself, bouncing through the office, all blond curls and huge smile, shouting good-natured urgencies at various people. But today Joe is out on the campaign trail when I scoot past his empty office, running the gauntlet of college kids in wrinkled khakis and stained Harvard and Yale T-shirts who peer up at me, bemused.

Although I am a fairly familiar sight around the office by now,

I continue to receive disconcerted looks, and I am never quite sure why. Sandy, a teenaged babysitter from my shadowy childhood days, unexpectedly moved to Southwestern Michigan just months before I left for Boston; she overflowed with stories of the high life in New York City and closets of semidesigner clothes, both of which she freely bestowed upon my sister and me. As I try to affect a casual stroll into the war room, I am equally grateful for her wardrobe and her society expertise, which I trust implicitly. Today, along with my habitual full-face makeup and four-inch-high bangs, I am wearing one of her Ralph Lauren blue-striped seersucker suits: blazer and skirt, pink T-shirt, and white pumps. I feel certain the look is Preppy Handbook-certified.

After what seems an interminable walk, I finally end up at Rory's desk where I stand awkwardly until she looks up. A few people around her sneak sideways glances. I am beginning to suspect that Sandy's ballyhooed East Coast experiences may have been with a radically different set than this pod of old money rumple and Hyannis Port slouch. Rory raises her eyes reluctantly, lingering a bit on my ensemble.

"Hi," I say brightly—frosted-pink smile, lacquered bang-bubble bobbing. I was never a cheerleader, but I bet I fooled the whole room in that instant.

Rory blinks at me.

I smooth my poufy skirt down around me, feeling acutely garish in the presence of her scuffed and rumpled prep school cool.

"Hi?" She regards me warily.

It is my first experience with that blank, self-protective look celebrities cultivate to keep mortals at arm's length when we cross their fragile fourth wall, barging into their lives uninvited. I know instantly that I am all wrong—this is all wrong—but I don't know how to fix it. We are momentarily unified, Rory and I, in our mutual horror at the weirdness of this encounter.

I manage to stammer that we're the same age and I don't know anyone else our age in the office, so I just wanted to say hi. Her look of surprise is very honest, but the subsequent sardonic grin cuts to the quick. "Really? I thought you were, like, twenty-five."

The conversation is clearly over.

Not sure how to leave, I end up chirping on repeat that I just wanted to meet the only other young person there before I scuttle out.

16

Humiliated and confused, I tried one more time to make friends, fit in, and overcome my inexperience with just about everything.

A week before I would leave was the culminating event I'd been working on for most of my time with the campaign: a big fundraiser party at a hotel in downtown Boston. Renowned jazz trumpeter Dizzy Gillespie was headlining, and it fell to me to chaperone him around town for the day and ensure he had everything he needed for his evening appearance, which of course secured the delicious obligation to work the nighttime event as well.

I myself did not know who Dizzy was. I had never heard jazz music, had never been to a cocktail party or a concert. I had never been to a real event of any kind.

The campaign event coordinator offered to arrange it so that I could spend the night in Boston afterwards, thus avoiding the long drive out of town past midnight. Mom found it within herself to agree, and I found out that it meant sleeping over at Rory's apartment where she and several other prep school classmates had taken up residence while working on the campaign. I didn't even know teenagers could have their own apartments, and I was entranced but terrified at this second chance to make worldly friends.

The day began auspiciously enough when I picked Dizzy up from Logan airport, ferrying him to campaign headquarters in my little Civic. A gregarious sort, he began to make genial small talk with me. I panicked momentarily as the enthusiastic, rapid-fire, deep-South patter bubbled up from somewhere between his legendary lungs and cheeks; I couldn't understand a word he said. But after a few awkward tries, I learned that asking him to repeat himself did nothing for my comprehension, so we settled into a smiling, nodding, pointing, laughing relationship for the rest of the day.

We dropped his bags at the evening's hotel, then hit headquarters where he was greeted excitedly by various Kennedys and campaign bigwigs. I made careful note of their excitement—this odd, old man with his beat-up trumpet case and impossibly unique speech must truly be a big deal if these mythical family members and tabloid favorites were so bowled over. I resolved to make Dizzy's time as pleasant and perfect as I could. I might not know how anyone in "the world" did anything, but I sure knew how to please and make things pretty and perfect.

Dizzy finished the meet and greet and indicated that he needed to cash a check. We drove around Boston, our communication problems further amusing him and horrifying me, and finally agreed on a bank. He received a few doubletakes as we entered, and soon a handful of overly helpful bank employees gathered around us with big grins. We were whisked into a glass-walled conference room, and dozens of people watched as Dizzy produced a crumpled check from his coat pocket and handed it to the banker, mumbling. She smiled, somehow effortlessly understanding what he was saying to her. He smiled back.

She asked for ID.

Dizzy began to pat himself down, first cavalierly and vigorously, then more slowly. Everyone stood around in increasingly awkward silence. A second, even slower pat down. A longer silence.

Alas.

Mr. Gillespie had arrived in Boston with no wallet and not a shred of identification.

I felt somehow responsible; he had been left in my charge for the day, and I wanted so badly to do it all perfectly. The dilemma also produced mild panic in the bank staff. They could not go against protocol, but they desperately wanted to avoid offending the legendary musician in their midst. They consulted amongst themselves.

Suddenly Dizzy grunted and lit up with a huge smile. He put a finger to his lips and blew. Instantly his cheeks ballooned out like spinnakers on dueling America's Cup challengers—billowing and pulsing, completely obliterating the lower half of his face and swallowing his ears. His eyes, now barely visible, twinkled gleefully.

The room burst into cheers and laughter.

Approximately ninety seconds later we were back in my car, cash in hand. From the bank we proceeded to the event hotel where Dizzy and I parted; he went to his room, and after I parked the car, I toted my bag to a room rented for event staff. Alone in the bathroom, I eagerly laid out two sets of hot rollers, a curling iron, various brushes and combs, a counter full of makeup, two cans of hair spray, white pantyhose, my white faux-leather pumps, and an ivory silk dress with big gold buttons, even bigger shoulder pads, and a super-wide belt. I was ready for the first real worldly party of my life!

Two hours later, curled, sprayed, ironed, and made-up to within an inch of my life, I sat stiffly at the bar making small talk with the campaign manager—a flirtatious recent Harvard grad whose parents owned a summer house next to the iconic Hyannis Port Kennedy compound. He offered to buy me a drink. I had already decided that if he asked me, I was going to sleep with him. I had only kissed a boy a few times, and I was only mildly attracted to him, but my time in "the world" was coming quickly to an end, and I did not know if or when I'd be free again. I had come all this way to experiment, yet so far I was still brimming with unwanted virginity.

It seemed wise to start with the drink.

In an odd moment of fear and honesty, I confessed I'd never

had a drink before. Judging by the resulting look on his face, my plans for virginity-shedding were not happening that evening. A reputedly voracious party boy, if you believed the gossip in the office, he seemed both overwhelmed and underwhelmed by my innocence and turned instantly into a very kind, protective big brother. He took my first-cocktail deflowering quite seriously, scrutinizing the bar menu and eventually selecting a fuzzy navel, which he told me shouldn't taste too much like alcohol. After paying for it and gently instructing me not to drink it too fast, he fled. I didn't see him again for the rest of the night.

But he needn't have worried about the drink. I took a single, mincing sip through the wee cocktail straw, barely wetting my tongue. It was syrupy sweet, with an underlying perfumy bitterness, as if I had licked a hairspray bottle. I assumed that was the alcohol.

I shoved the drink discreetly back to the bartender and immediately began monitoring myself for signs of drunkenness. As with everything else for which I had not been taught critical thinking skills, alcohol consumption was a black-and-white thing: even one taste, one whiff, was as bad as a bender. Just a sip was all the sin Satan needed to sink his hooks into me and work unspeakable horrors.

Obsessed with awaiting my alcoholic undoing as I was, I could barely carry on any conversation for the rest of the evening. At my door-greeting position, I checked and double-checked every name, pronouncing them as if I had just learned to read, thinking surely I would start slurring my words if I didn't enunciate louder and slower.

I watched Dizzy Gillespie get on stage, everyone cheering wildly when his cheeks did their thing. I had never heard jazz before. After the novelty wore off, the first song and the next sounded nearly identical to my untrained ears, and many others followed suit. I decided I did not like jazz.

I may have been thrilled to be there, but I was not enjoying myself.

Somehow I got through the night and drove in terror to Rory's apartment. Even though the pindrop of alcohol had been consumed four hours previously, I checked my rearview mirror the entire way, fearing the flash of lights indicating my drunken gig was up. I was so paranoid at that point, I don't remember entering the apartment—was anyone there? How did I get in? How did I know what room to sleep in? I removed my makeup and crawled into bed, praying that the phantom alcohol would wear off before morning and I wouldn't wake up with that indelible, possibly even irreversible, Satan-stain: the hangover.

The sounds of giggles and gossip in the living room outside my door jolt me awake in the morning. I lie carefully in bed for a moment, checking myself for signs of Satan's inebriation takeover. I'm not sure what to look for, but I feel fine.

I shoot out of bed, longing to join the fun outside, to make friends, but the idea to pop out in my pajamas au naturel never even occurs to me. I begin the long process of hair and makeup: hot rollers, hairspray, foundation, powder, contour, lip liner. I look furtively around while I wait for the rollers to cool in my hair, visually cataloging how the room's owner lives. I know it belongs to Max's girlfriend, Max being a particularly cute brother of Rory's. I met him at one point over the summer, recognizing him instantly from the striking black-and-white photographs I saw in *Interview* magazine a couple years ago.

The room doesn't display any of the accoutrements I would associate with the girlfriend of a sexy guy pictured in *Interview*. The room is bare; scraps of paper, a few books, balled-up jeans, and faded T-shirts are strewn about, the closet empty of any wardrobe requiring hangers. And why would she be gone—off somewhere on a trip, I'm told—instead of here, catering to her famous boyfriend? How do these girls get boys to like them without the piles of makeup, the hair styling, the ironed and dry-cleaned wardrobe? What about the obsequious obedience? What value do boys find in them if they are off doing their own thing instead of being at his beck and call? I am deeply mystified.

The warm and bawdy conversation outside ceases the instant I open the door decked out head to toe in my best. Rory and two other young women in indistinguishable, rumpled cotton coziness stare at me, cigarettes and coffee cups in midair. I stare at the room. It is piled high with takeout containers, clothes, dirty plates; a haze of smoke brushes the ceiling. We all stammer a good morning.

To her credit, Rory makes an attempt at hostessing, asking if I'd like anything. I ask if they have eggs and cheese and offer to make everyone an omelet. They look at me, startled and politely amused. No, they have no eggs. They don't really eat breakfast.

As they suck down Marlboro reds and douse them in last night's beer bottles and we all absorb the awkwardness, I am acutely aware that they are thoroughly appalled at my midwestern inexperience and earnestness. My mall bangs and heavy makeup. Worse, it suddenly hits me that, unfailingly gracious as she is, Rory must be dreadfully embarrassed to have me in her space, to have to explain my existence in her world. I am an acute embarrassment not only to myself . . . but to her.

Who I am is all wrong, yet again. I remember my only appearance with Joe on the campaign trail—dancing at an old-folks home. How I had obsessed over what to wear, finally choosing a turquoise one-piece jumpsuit with shoulder pads, an elastic waistband, and big hair—something I had figured was perfect, a straight-up Cars music-video vixen. Followed by my disastrous friend-making attempt in a suit and heels. And now I stand before them in pink polyester-blend plaid and white heels, my bangs nearly high enough to catch in the overhead fan.

My wrongness is yet again terribly painful and confusing, but I don't know how to fix it. I have been valued only for my looks all my life—*these* looks—these artificial, exaggerated, feminine looks that are suddenly so garishly off the mark. That is all I have.

And I can make an omelet, and I can clean a house.

These prep school girls sprawled before me with bare faces and shaggy hair clearly have none of that. They don't need any of it. They have something else.

Of course, they have money, they have names, they have cool. But more than that, they know who they are. They have had at least one person, institution, or system in their lives that has told them they are okay just the way they are, that their value lies in themselves.

They are not trying to be pleasing. They are not trying to gussy up, shut up, and back down, not trying to fit and accommodate and reduce themselves according to someone else's wishes. They are not serving and performing.

They are come-as-you-are, and they are taking up space. They are real. And they are okay with that.

Astoundingly, everyone else seems to be, too.

I slink out of the apartment mortified, confused . . . and very impotently envious. My mother and I make the fourteen-hour drive home to Michigan two days later, and I begin my senior year at the Adventist Academy.

It is not an easy reentry.

17

Back in the smothering grasp of Adventist school after my glimpse of freedom and a totally different way of teening, I felt more trapped than ever. Even if I knew how to get the confidence and effortless cool of Rory and her friends, I was locked into my rigidly maintained looks and manners—none of which had ever belonged to me. They belonged to anyone and everyone else who wanted to weigh in. I was controlled by my pastor, my teachers, my principal, my parents. It all belonged to them and God and Ellen White.

So I doubled down on the only thing I knew I could control. I could do what I wanted with the meat of me, the frame on which everyone hung their projections and expectations, that evil flesh housing which could be perfected and made to perform on the surface—leaving the underneath for me to ruin how I pleased.

I could control what I did with that body. I could control how much I ate and how much I moved. That was the bargain I had to make in order to keep my family and community pacified: they could control everything about my life except those secret physical degradations I could pull off right under their noses. So I could and would continue starving and exercising and injuring myself—biting and ripping off my cuticles, tearing the skin off my lips, pulling my hair out methodically—until I bled, until I could feel.

And I could have sex.

I turned all of my attention senior year to sex. The morality of it never crossed my mind. I had internally rejected all Adventist teachings a while ago, but as with all things requiring introspection and self-knowledge, it was unclear exactly when or how I had done so and what I had replaced the system with. At best I suspected I had actually never believed any of it in the first place; I'd just been terrified of Hell and disappointing others. Then I figured if I'd never had faith, I wouldn't need to replace it with anything. I must just be morally hollow, ethically bereft.

I must just be bad.

I knew I had to carefully guard my heretical leanings, however, until I could escape for good, so that fall I doubled down on my pious demonstrations: leading Sabbath School, weekly chapel skits, Week of Prayer volunteering, Honor Society, community outreach programs. I smiled, I prayed, I churched, I sang. I was modest, pleasant, and pleasing as hell.

But my naughty body and dirty, dark human soul—so full of original sin and born evil? That untrustworthy, wayward female form that was so dangerous that I could not be trusted to police myself, so everyone else had to do it for me? Those rebellious parts were hell-bent on adventuring, no matter what the risk. And they refused to wait until I graduated.

So I went on the hunt. On Sundays I started reading the local sports page at the library and scrutinizing the athletes at the local public high school. It didn't take much study before I made my pick: our dinky town had been improbably graced by a pair of beautiful Greek twins, Nick and Alex Markopoulos: superstars in nearly every sport, with muscles and bone structure worthy of any classical sculptor, gorgeous olive skin, and big dark eyes. I learned from my cousin, who had liberal, Adventist-lite parents and attended the public school herself, that Nick was reportedly less devoted to his girlfriend than Alex.

I checked out both girlfriends. Not only was Alex apparently very stuck on his girlfriend, but she was also extremely pretty. I clearly had a better chance against Nick's. And so it was decided, just like that: Nick would be the recipient of my virginity.

My campaign began in earnest.

It was fairly believable to my parents on Friday nights when I suddenly claimed I would be attending Academy vespers, the first of three church services within our twenty-four-hour Sabbath. Instead of showing up at the school chapel on Friday nights, however, I veered off to the public school football games a few miles out of town.

My initial efforts were massively disappointing. As much as I thrilled at feeling finally a bit like a normal teenager—*Friday Night Lights*! Football! On the *Sabbath*!—the whole confusing scene was too spread out, too chaotic, and way too dark for productive long-distance seduction. I couldn't figure out how to even get close enough to the action to make any of the players notice me, and they didn't take their helmets off long enough for me to get a good look at them, either. I fumed for many chilly nights under the dim stadium lights, swaddled in shapeless cold-weather gear. It was impossible to clinch a conquest from afar in a parka.

But in January, basketball season brought perfect star-athlete hunting conditions: infinitely more flattering indoor apparel for both me and them, under bright lighting, in confined quarters. I wore the brightest red or hot pink shirts I could find, aligned myself in the stands wherever the Berrien Springs bench had a direct view, and I locked eyes with whichever twin glanced my direction at any given moment.

I lingered in the stands after games just a bit longer than most attendees. I figured out where the bus parked and made sure I just happened to be parked nearby, standing casually outside of my car. I did not have time for subtlety.

Finally, a stroke of luck: my cousin told me Nick had a job at the local taco stand, a tiny cement hut on the corner of our single stoplight intersection. The next Saturday I waltzed in and ordered a burrito after church. I wore a 1940s black outfit of my grandmother's: a spectacular jewel-encrusted skirt that flared open to reveal hot-pink accordion pleats, a fitted, off-shoulder velvet top, and long satin opera gloves. Perfectly sprayed curls reached halfway down my back, not to be outdone by my full Vogue-worthy '80s maquillage. With a hat. With a veil and feather.

Even *I* knew I was comically overdressed for a noon taco-hut visit at *the* stoplight. But I was betting on the fact that I was not too overdressed for starting a conversation and ending up without my virginity.

I was not wrong.

18

It is my father's birthday, and there are dark puddles of blood all over my parents' bed, messy splotches seeping into the petal-pink sheets that my mother pulls and burns and heats flat and smooth before forcing them onto the mattress. Tight and thin, the sheets are tortured into perfection and obedience just like everything else in the house—just like my body currently spread on top of them.

I don't know enough to be embarrassed or ashamed of the blood yet. Since periods are completely natural—happening to everyone with a uterus, taking up nearly one week of each month—and they virtually guarantee a pregnancy-free romp, I assume period sex is as common as jello at a church potluck. The idea that men would want or even be able to skip that week doesn't remotely occur to me. After all, Mr. Walsh hammered home that men's sexual desire and demand is righteously insatiable, a God-given drive that must be cheerfully, instantly, constantly satisfied by their chosen women, or else the shame and responsibility of a man's straying—his outsourcing to another—will be justifiably, directly laid at the feet of she-who-will-not-put-out. I am still blissfully naive to the millions of ways women can learn to feel bad about the millions of ways their natural bodies can fall short of men's sexual expectations—those desires they have that you can't fulfill, through no fault of your own, but for which you will be judged anyway.

I will learn all of that later.

Right now Nick and I are awkwardly Jackson Pollocking our way through my defrocking. We have only been together, if you can call it that, for a couple weeks, but I made sure he knew I am on the accelerated track, in the AP class with sex as with everything else. Not surprisingly, he did not object. For someone who could tally fewer kisses than fingers at that point, I learned to give a blow job amazingly fast. I was fascinated by the process. Nick expressed surprise that I swallowed. I have no idea what he means and am mystified that somehow there is another option. I also don't realize there is a reciprocal event until Nick mentions that he and his football buddies don't give oral sex, it's gross. I'm not sure what he's referring to there either, but I do take to heart that there is something apparently unsavory about my female parts. Oral sex for me is thus taken off the menu as soon as it appears there. But that's okay; I am not into wild experimentation or variety right now. I have a rigidly narrow focus, a one-point agenda. And here I am, on the cusp of graduating!

Nick is sweetly wary as we warm up, asking multiple times if I am quite sure this is what I want. He is clearly afraid I will freak out on him, like that girl everybody knows with the really long hair who theatrically insists on getting a pixie cut and then afterwards screams and cries in a ball on the floor for hours and won't go to school for weeks.

I laugh and assure him I am not that girl, nor will I imprint on him like a baby duckling and insist that God has made him my husband. So we proceed, a bit mechanically.

He is gentle and slow. Kind but still hesitant. Does he feel an overwhelming responsibility to make sure my first time is good? It never occurs to me that his hesitancy might be him hoping, waiting, inviting me to participate in some manner. I know I am supposed to enjoy it, which I try self-consciously to express, but to actually display agency or action, to express any needs or desires of my own, is way above my pay grade.

I have never spent so much time in my parents' room. It is not forbidden, necessarily, but it is definitely not inviting. For the first time I realize, looking around, that it is a bewilderingly girlish, feminine space, with a cabbage-rose comforter and curved, white furniture. I cannot picture my father in this room.

I shudder, shake my head clear—I do not want my thoughts to go there! For someone who has learned to covertly plan everything in her life, ending up in their bedroom hadn't crossed my mind. It just so happens that my parents have taken their only joint, kidless trip in my memory together to California to celebrate Dad's birthday. This has worked out to be a crime of opportunity.

I am brought back to the task at hand when Nick asks if it hurts. I am stumped. I have no idea, honestly, and I couldn't care less if it hurts. I am so excited that I can't feel a thing. It is not sexual excitement—I don't know what that is. It is a frenzied, godawful sense of escape, the release of everything pent-up and forbidden after so many years of choking on it.

I am not giving my virginity away. It is not a gift, and it is not being taken. I am giddily destroying it, tossing it aside, throwing it out. Determinedly, viciously ridding myself of it once and for all. This is the beginning of decades' worth of sex without desire or love: sex with a statement, sex with an agenda, sex with vengeance. The stupefyingly simple act is not just a rite of passage, it is the rage in me that will take years to work out.

But again, I won't know that until later. We finish with his orgasm. I feel so accomplished.

Lying back in the crimson-saturated embrace of permapress pink cotton, I wait for guilt. I wait for that huge, emotional love connection that is supposed to immediately form when I've "given myself away." I feel around for that piece they always warned would be ripped from my wholeness with each unholy union, leaving me in moral and psychological tatters.

I wait for something, anything.

Nothing.

We are silent.

But that's okay. This isn't about the experience or the feelings. It is about the act, just as with everything else in my life. The only meaning is in the performance, the achievement. And I have *done it*.

This act, this *thing* that was so huge, so fraught, so storied, so shamed and feared and forbidden—so managed and administered and ruled—*it doesn't belong to me*. There is nothing personal about it. It has been utterly depersonalized for years on end with so much management, so much baggage, so much moral weight and so many infinite rules.

And so I am simply, wildly proud of myself for having no feeling attached whatsoever.

I win.

I start giggling.

Nick looks concerned. He is undoubtedly head-gaming the teen sex-romp-movie playbook. Is the girl about to go psycho? Should he leave quickly? Is she laughing at him?!

No. She is not.

She is thinking about how the Israelites used to heap their sins on the head of a goat and then slit its throat in sacrifice on the temple altar. She is laughing because she herself has taken that great and most precious sacrificial commodity she has—the chastity and kept-ness of a Christian woman—and she has slaughtered it in her parents' bed, enlisting a heathen to help her bleed it out.

The bed sure ended up looking like someone died in there.

That was one way to look at it.

The next morning I felt like a new person, an alien. I had a secret. I was overflowing with self-confidence and independence—a whole new sensation, like nothing I had ever known. I had a *new* thing that only *I* could control, and they, all of them—Ellen White, my teachers, my parents—couldn't touch it, they couldn't take it away. They didn't know I had it. I had done and become what all the adults were so afraid of, what I had been punished for writing about, thinking about, just a couple of years ago. I had cracked their code, I had done the unthinkable, and I had proven that nothing bad would happen.

I skipped off to school brimming with sophistication, a huge smile on my face, reveling in the fact that I reeked with new adulthood, with forbidden sexuality. But as I radiantly whispered my achievement to my friends, our forbidding principal, Dr. Maines, approached.

I quaked. Did I give off a vibe *that* strong? My life—one dull litany of sinlessness culminating in one quick night's immorality—literally flashed before my eyes. Somehow God had ratted me out.

But Maines asked me instead to sit on the platform for morning devotionals, in front of the whole school, and perform the ending prayer. I spent the ensuing half hour of announcements, hymns, and sermonizing glowing, trying to beam out my sexual freedom to my peers, silently broadcasting my superiority to their purity problems. It was so *easy*, this leaving the religion, this shedding of its stupidity. Just look at me sitting here, safely out beyond its reach, completely over it. I grinned, thinking of the Egg White passages they had choked me on not even a year ago: "In no way, perhaps, is Satan more speedily accomplishing the utter ruin of a fallen and fast degenerating race than through the channel of unchastity and licentiousness."

And then I executed my most beatifically pious, high-performance prayer ever.

I was irrevocably, visibly changed. With a simple physical act—so easy, so uncomplicated, so seemingly lacking in meaning or weight—I had rejected forever the expectations of who I should be as a pure (worthwhile and valuable) Christian girl. That girl was gone, and I was now and forever a worldly, sophisticated woman. Sex didn't mean a thing. I had not lost anything, I had not given up anything, I had not felt anything at all except triumph and relief.

I was sure my peers must sense it, must see it, and would be thrilled I had proven there was nothing but freedom beyond the lies we'd been told. I imagined they would be admiring, in awe of my brave jump over the wall caging all of us. I expected respect and applause.

What I got was radically, awfully different.

19

Muhammad Ali's fist speeds past my face.

It stops beside my ear and slowly uncurls, ruffling the edges of my Michigan mall hair. Trembling on the thick palm is a crumpled red silk flower. A timid, childlike smile appears on Ali's famous features. Withdrawing the shaky hand, he begins with silent concentration to prepare his next magic trick: pulling a handkerchief out of his fist.

I am not quite sure why I am at Muhammad's house, except that I am brokenhearted over Nick—he never really stopped seeing that girlfriend, and he ditched me a couple months after our first tryst. I am in need of distraction and sympathy, and Matt Sanders is available. He's a casual friend of my sister's, and our families occasionally socialize together, but I don't know him well. He offered a diversion for the day, accompanying him on this odd business call, and I have gladly accepted.

My dad is Muhammad's doctor, but I am here today with Matt, who is busy trying to sell Muhammad on a signature line of sweatsuits. Matt is more well known in our town than the huge man seated across from him, but far less beloved. Muhammad inches slowly through town in a brown convertible Rolls Royce, smiling cherubically, handing out candy to kids. He speaks rarely and poses patiently for endless, monotonous photo requests: "Mr. Ali, can I get a picture? Pretend to knock me out! No, I'll pretend to knock you out!" And so it goes, a million pictures of the amiable giant being chucked slo-mo on the chin by some twit. In contrast, Matt rips around town in a series of bright sports cars, collaring friends and enemies alike into various investment schemes and scams. He can talk anyone into anything but never gives anything to anyone without expecting a lot in return.

Thus our sales-call date to Muhammad's legendary property, originally the safe house of Al Capone, who would allegedly jet across Lake Michigan when things got too dicey in Chicago and hide out amongst the meek Adventists. What better cover? But the grandeur I expected from the marriage of Scarface and The Greatest is sadly lacking. In fact, The Greatest himself is rather The Disappointing in my mind. I came for glamour, but there is just a gentle man in double-knit polyester with Parkinson's symptoms, surrounded by mismatched furnishings and bad pine paneling. Movement seems difficult and speech bothersome.

Which serves him quite well with Matt. When Muhammad has exhausted his repertoire of magic tricks, he simply stands up and leaves the room. Matt jumps up to follow, only to be intercepted by Ali's wife, Lonnie.

"He'll let you know," she says firmly, ushering us out the door.

Leaving empty-handed and embarrassed, Matt suggests that the two of us buy champagne and go to the lake. There are no liquor stores in our rabidly religious little village, so we drive to a remote town up the shore. After gallantly making our purchases—champagne for the lady, wine coolers for the gentleman—Matt drives onto the back roads.

"What beach are we going to?" I ask idly, sticking my feet out the window. I am more perturbed by the knowledge that Matt drinks wine coolers, the teenaged girl candy cocktail, than the fact that I have no idea where we are going.

Wind whips sand in our faces when we finally get out of the car. I hate the Midwest, but this is beautiful: bleak, rolling dunes dotted with brambly scrubs and swaying forests of reedy-looking things. Matt retrieves a blanket from his back seat and heads up a tiny, barely distinguishable path.

We wind through the bushes forever before Matt burrows into a particularly dense thicket. I expect the vista of a secret beach ahead of us, but the place is exactly what it appears: a little hollow beneath a bunch of weeds in a dip between sand dunes.

Settling on the blanket, Matt pops the champagne, and I launch into the sad details of my romantic failure with Nick. Drinking straight from the bottle, I soak up the alcohol and sympathy. Matt has never appeared to be a good listener before, but he seems really interested today.

I can hear the faint swish of petty lake waves in the distance. No crashing and rushing like an ocean, just the sedate little laps of a puppy tongue. If I were a lake, I think, I'd be embarrassed. Polishing off the champagne, I throw it unsteadily in front of us, watching its heavy roll downward in big, clumsy circles. My tale of woe winds down in similar ungainly loops, and Matt begins to reveal his own romantic past.

Tina, his girlfriend of four years, is devoutly Adventist and saving herself for marriage, or her hymen at least. He bitterly describes many "almost" moments in the years of chastity maintenance, but Tina and God always won out in the end. Matt is still an unwilling virgin. At least that explains the wine coolers, I figure. As I ponder an appropriate response to the revelation, a verbal Hallmark of suitable sentiment, Matt makes a move.

Next thing I know, I find myself sprawled on the blanket with Matt lying full-length on top of me. The change in position causes instant champagne mutiny, and I gag on frothy bile. Matt's body weighs heavily on my chest, pinning my shoulders with his. I stare, shocked, into the close-set pupils hovering above me. We are both a little cross-eyed.

I try to move, but he holds my arms beside my head. The squeak of sand under us seems loud and endless. His lips are dry and rough; he pecks at me fiercely, but with tongue—a weird, French peck.

"Matt, get the hell off of me!" I try to bury my face under my elbow. My head swims and my stomach lurches dangerously. I have only just started drinking recently, and I'm still a lightweight.

"I'm just trying to kiss you, what's wrong with that?"

I have both hair and sand in my mouth, but they are better than Matt's tongue or champagne redux.

"Come on. You've already had sex, what's the difference?" he barks. "Why can't you just have sex with me, too?"

"Matt. GET. OFF. ME!" I try to knee him in the groin, but his ankles wrap around mine. I begin to panic. If I offend him, how will I get home? I have no idea where we are.

"You're already a slut," he hisses. "You know you're going to Hell. Why don't you just sleep with me? Aren't we friends?"

Ah yes. I might as well eat the cookie since my diet is already ruined. I freeze, however, momentarily guilt-stricken. It is programmed into me: *I can't be a tease*. Women are responsible for the sexual urges of men. Our presence, our mere bodies are an overwhelming temptation. I can't be accused of leading men on; that would be harlotry, that would be an unfair tease.

Matt struggles to unzip his pants while pinning me with his pelvis and shoulders. It occurs to me that rape is probably not the easiest way for a guy to ditch his virginity.

Rape. Really? Matt is barely bigger than I. I am not going to be raped today.

With my left hand freed by his efforts to rally the Sanders family jewels, I shove him off of me.

"Shit!" He lurches off balance, still struggling with his belt. He wore a belt when planning a rape?

I scramble frantically backwards, dragging the blanket into messy ripples and jerking Matt over. He falls face to face with the bottles of wine coolers hidden neatly beneath the blanket in a row, untouched. I failed to notice he wasn't drinking a drop while he encouraged me to drain the champagne.

"That's fucking *pathetic*, Matt." Marching back towards the car, I ignore the plaintive excuses behind me. We get in, and Matt peels out, spewing dramatic sand jets in huge arcs behind us. At least his car is getting some.

He drops me at home with a half-assed apology, all fear of exposure and zero penitence. I drive straight to a party my sister is throwing for her college friends and start telling the story before I reach the kitchen. Turns out I am not the only one Matt has pulled this trick on. That night I learn Matt has taken a run at basically every girl in church rumored to have had sex. He may have even drugged one. He told another that he was "just testing her purity" to see if she was maintaining the required virginal standard.

The church has branded us harlots. After the first, one penis is as good as the next on our road to Hell. Our virginity equals both our value and our agency; "give away" the one, and everyone is entitled to the rest.

I break out in head-to-toe hives the next day, burning, itching red welts like the plague. Doctors can't figure out what is wrong with me. I assume perhaps I mistakenly touched poison ivy in my struggles with my would-be rapist. But why the sudden allover appearance?

They inject me full of cortisone, but the hives just get worse. I am a medical mystery, a very miserable one, for about a week before the hives finally subside, a diagnosis never reached.

It is the first of many times my body will protest when I do not have the words. Apparently, what I thought now belonged to me is more than ever subject to men's overview, opinions, and interference. I have not gained freedom or control over anything; I have only opened yet another painful door through which people will shame, guilt, and manipulate me.

I swallow the incident, believing it to be my fault.

20

After Matt's attempted assault, getting out was all I cared about.

I did try out another boyfriend out of boredom and residual, restless ambition. Brad was another surface-performer Adventist whose small town habits and goals guaranteed our relationship would not last past graduation, but he was infinitely more experienced than I was on the sexual scale, and I resolved to learn as much as I could before my departure. Whereas Nick had been all about standard missionary sex and blow jobs for the few months we were together, Brad and I jumped into classic experimental cheeziness. We copied the food play sequences from *9½ Weeks*; we toyed with bondage using the seatbelts of his old Chevy Blazer like an awkward scene from a kinky mechanic's garage calendar. And Brad showed me that not all men would sneer at performing oral sex. He was good at it. He liked it. And so did I.

So when he broke up with me not much more than nine and a half weeks later—and his reason was that I liked and demanded sex too much—it was intensely shameful and devastating.

I was unwanted for wanting sex.

No matter what I did with my body, it did not seem to be okay with men. They always won, they always had the power. I was scared, confused, and defeated.

I swore off any more carnal adventures until I was free of the Adventist chokehold. I was one semester away from graduating, from turning eighteen and finally being able to strike out on my own. After all the subterfuge and waiting, I could finally see the end of the tunnel. I threw my energies into that. But my chosen landing spot didn't work out like I wanted.

I had only applied to one college: Harvard. With their rejection letter in hand, no backup plan, and unrelenting church and family pressure to attend Adventist higher education, my parents and I compromised on the Adventist boarding school in Austria. I had heard European SDAs were more louche than the uptight American congregations, and the whole thing had a certain gloss and cachet that I figured I could leverage somehow in my unrelenting ambition to "make it" in the big world. If this would be as far away as I could run, I would abandon everything, even my own language.

Two months after graduation, my sister drove me to the airport toting two suitcases full of unstylish "travel clothes" my mother had painstakingly purchased from Banana Republic, as if I were going on a safari, not to a classical old country far more sophisticated than our Michigan backwater. Seminar Schloss Bogenhofen was an educational catchall basket for German-speaking Adventists, housing a theological seminary, a "gymnasium" (the Euro equivalent of a college prep school) for twelve- to seventeen-year-olds, and a German-culture program for English-speaking college students. Boys at Bogie were allowed pretty much free run of the campus, but I and the other girls were locked in the Madchenheim every night at nine.

Not to worry. Within a couple weeks of my arrival, I had firmly ensconced myself in the "bad girls" posse—a first for me—comprised of two adventurous Americans and one Austrian. During the week we were required to adhere to a strict schedule of devotions, church-going, academic pursuits, and kitchen chores—much like any Adventist Academy—but on weekends we were free to roam Europe with absolutely zero supervision.

And we did.

Staying at hostels and in church basements, we sashayed all over Western Europe, getting into mild trouble wherever we could. I picked up smoking with a vengeance, cheekily calling our precious contraband cigarette packs "prayerbooks" and lighting up with a cosmopolitan flourish that never ceased to please me. We went nightclubbing and hitchhiking and topless sunbathing. I slept with every attractive male who amused me. I sort of learned German. I discovered I loved drinking.

Emboldened by our weekend adventures, we began to get sloppy on campus: showing up drunk to class, passing flasks in church services. Our debauched parties locked in my dorm room bathroom at night were at first quietly overlooked by administration, until our bold requisitioning of a nearby farmer's ladder created an embarrassing neighborly dispute that could no longer be ignored. We frequently stole it, storing it in the attic and lowering it out a compliant underclassman's second-story dorm window after curfew. Shivering in our thin lycra LBDs, high heels in hand, we would sneak through the snow out to the road, where a townie would pick us up and take us drinking, dancing, and carousing all night.

The administration's machinations for kicking us out were soon in high gear, so I quietly quit after Christmas and headed home before they could officially oust me. I didn't want that on my record because by that point, six months into the school year, I had secured a spot in the freshman class at Hofstra University on Long Island, New York. I knew nothing about the school, but I didn't care—it was a short train ride to New York City, and it fit the bill for my ongoing plans to fulfill that long-ago, library-fueled goal: come hell or high water, I was going to be a model and an actress, with a side of Ivy League. As always, my plans had been laid and pursued in secret so that I was spared the scoffing that such an unlikely and unattainable combo would have inspired. I was dead-set on eventually matriculating at Barnard College, the women's college in New York City associated with Columbia University, and Hofstra was to be my stepping stone.

At Hofstra I was put into the international dorm, which made for many interesting friends. I tried pot, which made me dizzy and nauseous, smoking my first joint with the royal nephew of the king of Bhutan. I went clubbing with hipster Lycee Francais graduates. I did coke in the bathroom at Nell's with Dennis Hopper's (very, very young) girlfriend, rubbed elbows with Matt Dillon at the latest glam velvet-rope bar, and once more bumped into JFK Jr. and his bodyguard at a downtown dive bar. I giggled with Wallace Shawn through a raunchy performance by Penny Arcade.

None of the forbidden vices I diligently checked off appealed to me as much as sex. Most of my college friends slept with their conquests rarely and did not seem terribly interested in pairing up. They made out and fooled around and then moved on, something that I simply could not understand. I didn't get the degrees of sex—the fun of fooling around, the point of saying, "No, I've had enough, that's all." That would be "leading a guy on" and would make you the worst kind of woman. To my understanding, according to Adventist Marriage & Family class, once the foreplay had started in any way, it was all a straight line to the finish: male orgasm. I had never had any other sex education aside from Nick, the high school football player, and Brad, the guy who thought I wanted too much sex. And certainly neither of them, nor any of my fleeting subsequent partners, were going to point out that I was, indeed, entitled to the same smorgasbord they were or that I could, indeed, step out before the bill was paid.

So I continued to drive my body, just as I had in high school, into more and more painful situations, the more sexually sordid the better. No missionary position for this ex-preacher's kid! I began to crave and depend on the obliteration of being abused and hurt. I didn't know why, and I didn't ask. I thought I was being a wild rebel, a girl with a kink. And I went on defiantly checking off wild but unfulfilling sexual adventures, drugs, and drinking while somehow maintaining an honor-roll status at Hofstra.

I returned to school one morning in early fall straight from a coke-filled night at Nell's to interview for my Honors English program. Reeking of smoke, I sat in front of a panel of professors in a black leather jacket and motorcycle pants, babbling about God knows what, high as a kite.

I passed.

I applied to Barnard as a transfer student that spring.

I got in.

I had somehow, finally, successfully stutter-stepped my way into my Ivy League dreams. I moved into my new dorm in the thick of New York City action, surely on a straight path to a free and glorious future.

21

I am definitely not at Barnard for the feminism and girl power. If I had my choice, I would be at Columbia itself; it's more impressive. But after my failure with Harvard, Barnard is the ultra-cool alternative, my carefully plotted backdoor approach to an Ivy League degree and the all-important entrance to New York City that I have sought since I saw my first *Vogue* magazine.

Mom and Dad are apparently mollified by the women-only aspect, and the grand old campus and grand old white-people pedigrees don't hurt either. Mom even accompanies me on move-in day, unlike last year's scared and lonely Hofstra arrival all by myself when I took a cab all the way to Long Island from LaGuardia. She is so charmed by my shared room in one of the original old dorms—the ancient, wood-sashed bay window, clawfoot bathtub, and 1940s tile—that she is on her hands and knees with a razor blade scraping the tile clean when I meet my new roommate.

Posy is a bohemian-preppy sandy blonde with a nose piercing and classic East Coast ritz roots, from the kind of family that has a string of houses with names and assorted relatives in sidebars in history books. She could have been one of the girls in Rory's flat. I am awed by her and adore her immediately. Even better, she likes me too!

Our room, with its convenient position overlooking "The Quad," quickly becomes a late-night gathering place. Everyone else seems to have done their heavy drug experimenting in high school, notching up a few dead classmates and rehab visits along the way, and I have done my handful of drugs at Hofstra, so we settle into drinking and smoking cigarettes for our vices. Soon enough, our room can pass for something straight out of the "Nouveau Prep" article I memorized from *M, The Civilized Man* magazine: overflowing ashtrays, beer bottle college candelabra, statement posters, piles of mix tapes.

    I am deliriously happy to suddenly, unbelievably be among them now: the cool girls in the real world. I am accepted for the most part, though always on the fringe. A core group of prep-school friends still visits each other's many houses on weekends, their mothers bringing the whole group presents from exotic travels abroad, taking them all out to expensive lunches at storied NYC eateries when they sweep glamorously through town. I never quite achieve that level of "in," but I am thrilled nonetheless just to pass; I'm always slightly terrified that I'll be outed as a fraud. Surely someone will recognize that I do not really belong here and only managed to sneak in, faked it to the bottom rung of this rarified existence. Yeah, I have a few thin stories to tell about the Kennedys, Muhammad Ali, and Henry Kissinger, whom I introduced at a Michigan Economic Club meeting and traded goofy notes with throughout the dinner, but those are one-off encounters artfully contrived or desperately pursued. I have none of the nonchalance of the girls in my classes as they gather in our dorm room or bum a smoke in line at the cafeteria: these daughters of iconic writers, progeny of diplomats and governors, offspring of the rich and famous—these children of investment banks, grocery empires, movie theater chains—descendants of movers and shakers of all stripes from around the world who are so confident in their existence, in their right and reason to exist.

    So I work double time to identify and hide or change my tell-tale nobody-family, religious-freak signs. While my year at Hofstra was spent in a scramble to accumulate the been-there-done-that of basic drugs and sex, my style and attitude has remained largely unchanged, blending in remarkably well with the bridge-and-tunnel crowd on Long Island—Midwestern big bangs and hairspray were a cozy fit with the last-gasp '80s there.

At Barnard, however, it is a distinctly different story: Posy's prep-school scruff, *Grateful Dead* vibes, and a general grunge aesthetic rule. So I try to ditch the dramatic makeup, music video hair, and polyester-blend T-shirts and play a desperate, silent game of cultural catch-up during the reminiscences of proms at the Plaza, weeks on the road following the *Dead*. There is no internet, and neither the *Encyclopedia Britannica* nor all the books in the gorgeous Columbia Library can give me what I need. That would be a passing grasp of *Sesame Street, Charlie's Angels, Catcher in the Rye,* Malcolm X, and whatever it must feel like to hide your boyfriend's OD on ecstasy while visiting your uncle, the ambassador to Chile.

I do a lot of listening. And faking. I am good at that.

I could probably contribute something unique from my own experience and background instead of trying so hard to fit in, but I submerge it all. When the few people close enough to know about my religious upbringing reach out for help on Bible questions for World Religions class, thinking I am surely a slam-dunk CliffNotes cheat sheet in the flesh, I can't remember a thing. I can barely recall what books are in the Bible, can't relate a single story or explain a simple theological tenet or name a basic biblical character. I am so invested in trying to bury all the weird that it never occurs to me to develop the unique and interesting parts of myself. I am in low-key panic mode, after all; I don't have time or brain space to spend another second of my life on religious bullshit. I am completely *free* and will never give any of it another thought. Besides, I'm having way too much fun catching up in the real world.

I join the Columbia Student TV station and begin writing, producing, and acting in shows: an episodic film-noir spoof or a campus nighttime soap opera featuring a future mayor of a major US city. I get an ushering job at the Columbia theater, where I brush elbows with Sting and his actress wife, the Marsalis brothers, and other musical greats. I get a huge rush out of just sitting on the grass of the Quad, wandering the Columbia Library, smoking cigarettes on the famous *Ghostbusters* steps beside the Alma Mater statue, meeting friends for pastries and gossip at The Hungarian Café, or playing drinking games at the Cathedral Bar.

And then there is class. There are so many options, so many offerings, so many things to explore and ways to become a great new me. I agonize over trimming my class load down to manageable levels because I need at least a decade to take everything I want: Lesbian Literature! Death in Modern Fiction! Not to mention the even larger Columbia catalog wide open to us: Shamanism! Greek Tragi-Comedy Masters! Tibetan Buddhism with Uma Thurman's dad!

I have all my life wanted to become a scholar, but now I realize I can also become a thinker, and that is far more exciting. Thinking was effectively forbidden in Adventist school. At Barnard, they have whole classes and books about thinking—*critical* thinking, even. Derrida, where have you been all my life?

By the end of my first year, I can feel it deep in my bones: I am changing, learning, growing. I am just at the beginning of my quest to broaden my horizon, let down my guard, and open my mind, and it is a thrill like nothing I have ever experienced in my life.

Before we left for the summer, Posy and I lucked into the living situation of our dreams heading into our second year, the prime housing lottery pick: a huge, top-floor apartment across the street from the college, overlooking Broadway through its massive windows, with a black-and-white '50s kitchen and a marble fireplace.

It had been *the* posh campus party pad our first year, inhabited by a pair of cooler-than-cool, designer-clad, multilingual brunettes. They hosted a staggeringly chic mix of Barnard/Columbia students, Eurotrash hipsters, and momentarily white-hot "it" models and actors like Uma (her father a cult figure in his own right at Columbia). It was an unbelievable coup. Posy and I were ready to assume campus party queen duties, and life could not have been better.

That summer we stayed at the Upper East Side apartment that Posy's art dealer dad kept for his artists. There I learned who Gaudi was when I left a red wine ring on the marble top of his dramatic gold-and-white mirrored settee. I also signed up for a science course, Rocks for Jocks at Columbia, since the pass/fail summer school scoring was better for my GPA and thus imperative for my long-term goals: earn great grades and go on to grad school to become an academic.

My mother, unable to give up the struggle for control, demanded that I come home immediately once the geology class was over. The unspoken agenda was clear: she wanted me to enroll in Adventist college to meet a suitable husband. I didn't want to come home. I had finally signed up for an acting class, gotten a headshot, and found an agent. I had a cocktail waitressing job at the hottest nightclub in town, the kind where people had secret passcodes and keychains to get past the velvet ropes and hobnob with the rock stars, movie legends, and supermodels sitting at my tables. I was well on my way to fulfilling every single one of my high-flying goals!

But Mom was not impressed with my dreams nor with the effort I had put in to achieve them. It all horrified her, so she resorted to emotional and financial blackmail: holding my education hostage much as she had my sister's years earlier. In a fit of desperation and anger, she announced that I was completely ungrateful for the education she'd been paying for—even though I had done nothing but appreciate and enjoy that education, draining every drop

I could get out of it and getting stellar grades. This clearly wasn't what it was about; I knew that, even if she did not. The problem wasn't me or my appreciation for my schooling, it was that *she* didn't appreciate my education. She greatly feared it. She feared she was losing me, that the family was losing me, the church was losing me.

My maternal grandparents had always paid for all of our education, so Mom was in control. But didn't my dad have anything to say? Didn't my grandparents want to see me finish the degree they had so far generously financed? They weren't talking, they weren't stepping in. I felt abandoned at my mother's mercy yet again, and before I could mount my own defense, she withdrew me from Barnard. Just like that, my college experience, with its attendant intellectual, emotional, social, and human growth, is over forever.

The intoxicatingly foreign liberation and intellectual challenge. The glamour, the self-development, the self-reliance. The boundary expansion, the limit explosion. The independence. The critical thinking. The progress toward tolerance and acceptance, the embrace of political and social justice. The exposure to and influence of strong, smart, driven women.

All gone.

22

I sob hysterically for weeks, mourning the loss of my wide-open future, my incredible education, my beautiful junior-year glamour pad—my entire future life as I had carefully planned it for over a decade.

But I am not going back to Michigan. Not now, not ever. Mom underestimates me—I survived her beatings and I will survive this, too. Financial deprivation and manipulation may have worked with my sister, but they will *not* work with me.

I inform my mother that I am not coming home, and I disappear.

Hopes for my brain dashed, I pour every ounce of my anger and terror into the only thing I know I can use: my looks. Coming face-to-face (or, more accurately, face-to-rib cage) with Elle MacPherson and Kate Moss and Karen Mulder and Helena Christensen every night while cocktail waitressing, I quickly realize I have no hope of becoming a major model; I am way too short and can only pass for averagely pretty. But I scrounge up little jobs, posing for subway public service posters, a local plumbing company's sale flier, a Macy's countertop perfume video. I couch surf with friends, I continue waitressing, and I start combing the pages of BackStage for auditions and castings.

It is a rough existence. I sometimes walk the length of Manhattan after auditions because I can't afford a subway token back to a friend's apartment. I go hungry on the days I have no waitressing shifts. I live day to day, moment to moment, starving and scared.

But I refuse to go home. I *refuse* to give in.

I am a terrible actor. I am only good at pretending, not feeling. I have no idea how to access my own emotions, let alone how to flesh out a fictional character. I try to imitate actors I love who fill notebooks for each character, carefully building out their entire history: how their mother held them as a child, how they prefer their coffee, how they receive an unexpected visitor, how they arrange their medicine cabinet, or what happened to them as a child that scarred them for life. I don't know any of this stuff about myself, however, so I have no idea how to get there for either me or my character. I end up merely aping the emotions that I know are appropriate. The camera sees through me more often than not; my acting is shallow, clunky, performative. But despite my severe emotional blind spots, I score several NYU and Columbia student films, then finally an independent feature—something I am very proud of, yet still a bitter recompense for losing my treasured spot at Barnard.

Days after our first shooting for an NYU film, I move in with one of the actors, a man twelve years my senior whom I of course slept with on the first day we met. Out of both sheer necessity and childhood programming, I immediately assume the identity of an attentive and obedient pseudo-wife, a role I will fulfill blindly and a pattern I will have trouble shaking for more years than I know. After six months, terrified at my disappearance and subsequent life trajectory into a "life of sin" with an older man, my mother caves. She allows me to re-enroll at Barnard.

But it is too late.

Posy has moved on, subbing another roommate into my space at the glamour pad over Broadway. I am a townie now, a "day student" with a nearly middle-aged de facto husband, and an absolute cipher on the academic and social scene. Emotionally and practically tied to living far off campus with my much older boyfriend, I'm deprived of on-campus camaraderie, social opportunities, clubs, and identity.

I live the meek domestic life of a dowdy commuter. My boyfriend and I have no mutual friends; we do not socialize. I ride the subway uptown—Barnard is nearly an hour's ride from our Tribeca loft—I go to class, and I immediately take the train home.

In order to make up for the lost semester and still graduate on time—in a desperate, obsequious scramble not to cost my mother any more money for an action she herself has taken—I trim down my academic loads to the bare minimum, taking only the necessary classes. Derrida is left unexplored; creative writing is too frivolous, philosophy is ditched. Dreams of going on to a PhD and becoming a professor go out the window. I dutifully tick off requirements each subsequent semester of my junior and senior years, filling them with the classes that fit my commuter schedule instead of the ones that truly fire up my heart and mind, until graduation arrives.

In my official Barnard photo from that ceremony on a bright May day in 1992, there is one tiny, brief victory—one that I cling to in memory; the photo itself is too painful to look at.

I am a happy graduate, long hair streaming back out from under my tasseled cap, striding into the diploma handshake with a huge, beaming smile. A smile of relief. Of sadness. And of vindication. I know at that moment that my mother is fuming out there on a plastic chair in the sun. She has sat uneasily through the ceremony held along Broadway, out of her comfort zone and distinctly unhappy. She is not proud of her daughter for graduating with an Ivy League diploma, its gilt lettering in Latin; not thrilled to be in the bosom of a major international city, not impressed by the revered institute of learning where she sits, not interested in the storied families around her, and not happy to be celebrating the achievements of brilliant and ambitious young women from around the globe.

No.

She is resenting all of those things for corrupting her daughter: a wayward girl who dared walk on stage to receive her certificate of completed higher education with ugly, stick-straight hair.

23

I stayed in New York City after graduation to pursue my unfinished dream of becoming an actor. A month after I got my diploma, I left my live-in older boyfriend for Andrei. I met him on a steamy, rainy summer day in the city, one of those rare, thunderous, black-sky-and-swirling-trash backdrops that makes you believe in Batman.

That particular day, I believe in everything.

It is my twenty-first birthday, and I have just aced a soap opera audition. I bounce out of the subway at Twenty-Third and Seventh Avenue into the diminishing storm, a defensive Walkman clamped onto my head. Most of the time it isn't on; I just use it as a way to pretend I'm not affected by the frequent street heckling and harassment. Today, however, I am listening to my favorite mixed tape, "Women with Muscles, Kickin' Booty," the cassette filled with overwrought feminine anthems so many times revisited that Janis Joplin is starting to sound like Alvin and the Chipmunks.

Striding over the steaming sidewalks, I hum along to "I Need You," my favorite Annie Lennox ballad of torment and torture. What more do I need to complete my birthday? I look up and see the sign above a liquor store: *karate*.

I have wanted to take martial arts for as long as I can remember. It's quite like my beloved gymnastics and all the forbidden dance lessons of my childhood—but with violence! I am a bit of an authenticity snob, however: I didn't want to study with some Michigan-local, self-designated guru who invented his own style from a hodgepodge of kung fu, tae kwon do, and origami. I want a *real* sensei—someone from the old country, someone experienced and wise who has devoted his life to a single ancient classical art.

Or, barring that, someone just like the man who stands motionless behind the curved wooden counter in front of me, wearing a blood-stained gi and a scowl.

On impulse I slipped upstairs past the glass bottles towards the flag with a dragon on it, but when I step into the hushed, glossy, wood-paneled atrium, I become acutely aware of my soggy self thinly draped in a cheap red halter dress damp from the storm. Dripping and underclad in what was a brilliant choice for a soap opera audition—short skirt, plunging neckline, exposed back—I am distinctly out of place in this whispering center of Zen violence.

The scowling man at the desk is quintessentially tall, dark, and handsome, with the classic Mediterranean features I adore—strong nose and flashing brown eyes—set against shockingly creamy skin. He asks if he can help me. Actually, it is hard to tell whether he has spoken since he barely moved his lips. Zen ventriloquism.

The black belt around his waist is ragged, more gray than black, little strings tangling along the double-wrapped width. His crisp, quilted cotton uniform is not as white as it appeared from the doorway; it embalms large, ancient, yellow shadows of sweat under the arms, a carefully patched rip on one shoulder . . . and is that *blood* on the left sleeve? A *lot* of blood.

The Walkman around my neck still pounds Eurythmics into my collarbone, Annie Lennox plaintively looking for someone to crack her skull, someone to kiss.

I stammer my request to sign up without checking to see if the echoey dojo room contains any experienced, wise, classical teacher. But I have found something I want more. I need the black-haired, pale-skinned man of indeterminate accent and big, dark eyes who wears dried blood with a smirk.

I throw myself into workouts from the first day onward, enthusiastically embracing the bloody-knuckle pushups and showcasing my leftover gymnastics flexibility in the deep, low stances and high kicks of *kata* routines. The day I am finally able to discipline myself to sit in *zazen* meditation until my feet go numb is a proud moment.

The only part I dread is fighting. Hyperventilating and trembling, I enter *kumite* class paralyzed by the prospect of direct confrontation. My first fight has to be halted because I am timidly throwing punches into the air, carefully avoiding any actual contact with my opponent. Once punches start landing, I often end up on my knees, heaving—not from being hit but from facing another person so directly. Forthright displays of aggression absolutely paralyze me. Losing is much preferred to winning. Pain is better than honesty. Anything is better than expressing forbidden, ugly emotions in a face-off.

Our dojo in a dirty-chic part of town attracts a glamorous crowd during the day: cocktail waitresses like me, trust fund babies, designers, directors, porn stars, artists, dancers, actors, and models of varying degrees. Through whispered locker-room gossip I learn the competition for my teacher's attentions is formidable, including an established soap actress and several models. But I'm not worried. I have an edge over the towering glamazons and daytime sexpots: I know what he needs. I saw the look in his eye when he first threw me onto the mat. And sure enough, only weeks after my first belt promotion ceremony, I gain entry into Master Andrei's personal life.

He invites me over for drinks, then throws me against the wall. Pinned to the two-tone gray paint of his posh downtown apartment, I forget what's happening and briefly thrill to the ultra-hip address. Master Silent might dress like he's never heard of fashion, but he has a great pad. Sandy, one of the models in the 10 a.m. basic technique class, has been seeing him casually, but tonight I fully intend to render her as obsolete as last September's *Vogue*.

I arrived, trembling, with a small gift. I wasn't sure what to get him, having still only exchanged a handful of words, so I settled on a Japanese-looking candleholder that I planned to explain was for meditation. But Andrei opens the door and wordlessly grabs me by the throat, yanking me into his front hallway and slamming me hard. The package flies out of my hand, hitting the floor with a tinny clang, and I imagine the little pagoda bent and crushed inside the tissue paper.

He lifts me onto my toes, crushing my lips into my teeth as he approximates a kiss. His mouth is loose and sloppy as he sends his tongue against mine; there is no cozy seal between our lips. I immediately know he neither cleans his spoon when eating nor gives good oral sex. Oral attention and control are easily identified by the condition of a spoon, and based on the way he is kissing me, he would definitely be the sort to leave streaks of food behind. I am disappointed but unsurprised. And distinctly unaroused.

My feet are off the floor, but I am on sure ground in this kind of moment.

Responding to the slobbery lip-lock while his hand tightens around my windpipe, I bite his tongue. Hard. I taste blood: elusive, hot, salty. I savor it with some of my last remaining conscious thoughts, the thick, red ooze pervading my mouth and vision at once.

"I like the way you play," Andrei mutters thickly, releasing my neck and swooping down to scoop me up. I fall unsteadily into his arms. I wonder what is going to happen next, like it's happening to someone else.

He carries me over the threshold of the bedroom, bride of Master Sadist, and throws me onto the bed. Grabbing my hand, he yanks me toward him, across the bamboo-print duvet cover, and quickly reverses the roll of my body, flipping me onto my stomach. I take note of the masterful Aikido move: he is using my own momentum against me.

He holds both of my wrists behind my back, crossed together

in one of his palms, and begins to disrobe both of us with his other hand. The pressure of his knuckles into my spine is excruciating. He leans harder into me. I can feel his uneven breath on my ear.

My neck burns as I strain to look at the Buddha on the small altar over the bed.

Are there seven circles of Hell . . . or Heaven?

24

Sex had everything to do with Heaven and Hell for me, naturally.

Ever since that first Nick romp, I had pursued ever more transgressive, wild, frantic, violent sex. The movie *Blue Velvet* had been a lightning bolt revelation: the close-ups of Isabella Rossellini's damp red lips begging to be hit, whispering that the poison had been put in her. Like her, I too had urged bewildered Kyles—wide-eyed, pasty-skinned young Griffins and Spencers and Blaines—to hurt me, beat me, bruise me, bite me. It was exciting, it turned me on, it fed something deep in me. It rarely led to orgasm, but I didn't care. I was after the obliteration of the soul that had been put in me, not sexual satisfaction. With each sexual humiliation, each degrading exhibition of sexual deviance, I was sure I had taken back the biggest, baddest female power and sin: I was proving I was free of the church and its archaic repression of women. I was fetishizing it, making it kink, see?

My own satisfaction never occurred to me. No one ever told me I was entitled to female sexual pleasure. Sex with men was only about men. Certainly nothing had ever shown me that sex equals love; after all, there was no sexual love demonstrated in the Bible other than Songs of Solomon, which our Adventist teachers and handlers had always dismissed as purely allegories for God's love for his bride, the church (which was, on reflection, a truly bizarre attempt at diversion, but apparently it worked with us). Biblical relationships were all transactional and unequal, all controlled by men administrating the possession of women: David creeping on and raping Bathsheba and killing her husband to have her; the Levite giving his wife to a city of men to rape; Rachel and Leah's father playing games with a man in order to pawn them both off and get fourteen years of free labor in the mix; Esther's uncle prostituting her to the king to save her people. The Bible amounted to a male sadist's wet dream and a blueprint for perfect masochism as a woman: submit, be abused, be traded, be raped; sacrifice yourself, your children, your loves, your life. And for our Seventh-day Adventist prophet Ellen White, sex was just wrong, all wrong, all of it. It was something so dangerous and destructive and uncontrollable that, according to her belief that spices inflame "base passions," even a squirt of French's Dijon could suck a girl right down the drain of promiscuity and into the sewer of sin. As for what few movies I had seen? Female pleasure was just a performance, all for the viewer—or the man, though usually one and the same.

 I only knew how to aim for overachievement and pleasing others, so I went big with sex like everything else. Sex was just sex was just sex, no meaning whatsoever, so I made it the most impersonal, performance-oriented, transactional deed—the most tightly, violently controlled sex ever. And I gave that control entirely over to someone else.

 It was New York in the early '90s; sex was everywhere in every variety. Everyone you knew was into something. You didn't even have to experiment yourself, you could just absorb it from others. Even in my (still!) somewhat sheltered experience, I knew—or knew people who knew—high-end escorts, dominatrices, and members of dungeons. I knew instinctively I did not want any of that. I did not like the Hermes silk scarves bondage that was popular in my social circle, nor did I want the leather-and-ball-gags at sex clubs and dungeons. It all seemed inauthentic. Oddly, even hilariously, in hindsight, I found all of that too performative.

 I needed the literal slave/master relationship depicted in the erotic novel *The Story of O* and, in the stories of the Bible: women given and taken, used, defiled, and utterly dehumanized. I sought to evolve the Stepford wife I had been raised to be—a high-functioning trophy, but with a dark underbelly of real, desperate physical pain and psychological ownership intended to crush your whole soul. I didn't want safe words. I needed to know I might quite possibly die with each sexual act. I deserved it. Sex was bad and so was I.

I could beat them at their own game, all those early controllers of every inch of my body and mind. I made a fetish of letting people hurt me more than they ever could. I had so smugly, wittily co-opted that servile, biblical woman into something deviant and dark, wickedly sexual, and I knew I could do it bigger and better. I could get an A+, I could overachieve—watch me go!

If my body was in pain, then I didn't have to feel or think. After all, the word "obey" had been since earliest memories not a verb but a way of life—my life—a forced abnegation of self so complete that all emotions, needs, and hopes were secreted away where even I couldn't find them anymore. To obey was the only freedom I knew.

The problem was that when your goal is to obliterate yourself by bodily donation to someone else's darkest desires, being choosy would be the ultimate oxymoron. I had all I needed with Andrei, the first genuinely sexually domineering man I found, so I stopped looking. He was surly, intense, and exotically different from anything in my world, and he hurt me. I had always been flatly disinterested in the preppy white boys who grew up like me—the wannabe Gordon Gekkos, the theatre snobs, the earnest academics. Even when I moved up in adulthood into the circles where they were bonafide millionaires, movie stars, and Rhodes scholars, they still left me cold.

But Andrei's allure was endless. His mother had once stabbed him in a petty squabble in the kitchen. He didn't speak to his dad, who only wore wife-beaters, chain smoked, and yelled instead of talking. Various family members were in pre-, post-, or present incarceration related to mob activity. They all lived on top of each other in a crumbling brownstone in the inner city, where there were children sleeping on couches and floors, and when you shut the bathroom door, it swung with the weight of twelve bathrobes hanging on the back. They had rosaries and godparents and confirmations and confessions and catechisms and all those forbidden sins that I'd been raised to fear as the signs of the Devil in *those Catholics.*

And they had those New York accents.

I was madly in love with being in love with him. It felt like I'd entered another world—exciting, illicit, far from how I was raised. And I was all about getting as far away as possible, of course.

Andrei and I were soon spending every possible waking hour together. After working so hard to get a toehold in the glamour industries, into my coveted Ivy League life, I abandoned it all for Andrei within the space of a few months. He scowled disapprovingly at my silly ambitions, so I scrambled to gain his favor by taking an "adult" eight-to-five office job working as a secretary for a hedge fund. This left me no time to audition or even for my beloved martial arts. I had several bosses that I adored, but the position utterly demoralized me. Going from goals of learned academia and big-screen movie stardom to booking flights and filling out expense reports for other people living their own dreams was excruciating. I was too tired after work and too deeply ashamed of my typing-pool status to even try to see my friends anymore.

This prison I created for myself worked exceedingly well for Andrei because, as thrilled as I was to enter his foreign realm, he distinctly did not return the favor. Not only did he disfavor my ambitions, he also disliked my friends, my family, my joys, my habits, my wardrobe. I had moved to a lovely apartment in the still-funky East Village, but he hated the city, so I moved into his condo in the boroughs. But it turned out he loathed that place too because it reminded him of his ex-wife, so he sold it, and we rented a house in a summer beach community—in the winter, far down on the deserted Jersey Shore, in a tiny town without even a restaurant or a movie theater. The move required a cold, draining, two-hour commute into the city each day and then back again—biking to and from the train station in the dark, switching trains midway on a deserted, perpetually windy platform—that turned my already grim work grind into a sixty-hour week.

Whenever I became disgruntled, Andrei would guilt me darkly about his terrible childhood, and I would immediately flood him with support. I could be the perfect helpmeet! I doubled down on trying to please him, to make it easier for him. What a burden he bore; how miserable it must have been for him to navigate the world with such crippling issues. It was the least I could do.

Andrei soon fixated on leaving the tristate area altogether. I still loved New York City; I wanted to stay there indefinitely, but Andrei insisted we move out West (avoiding anywhere near my extended family, which for generations had multiplied all over the Pacific Coast). We ended up in a basement apartment on the outskirts of Los Angeles. Andrei took a job in high tech, and I worked as a textbook editor.

He was obsessive about togetherness, both in our future plans and our physicality. He insisted that there was no reason to be a couple if we weren't together *all* the time, every day and night. Any hours outside of work we had to be in one another's company, or else it was pointless to even have a relationship, and he became hyper-focused on his new plan for our future: to save money and move out into a prepper-style environment, far away from civilization.

Our basement hovel was a symbol of the stringent savings plan he established. It had no furniture—we sat and slept on the floor for more than a year while horrified friends and family quietly gifted us furniture and appliances. We recorded every penny flowing in or out, even the change found on the road, in an Excel spreadsheet. We did not eat out, go to movies, buy anything, do anything. We did not have a car. We biked everywhere, rain or shine, balancing groceries or laundry on our handlebars. We had no TV. We dumpster dove for fun.

Andrei *could* be incredibly charming and humorous, the life of the party, for his work. He could turn on a high beam sarcastic wit at his dot-com company's high profile events, but for events at our sparsely furnished home with my friends or family, he was consistently surly, silent, hostile. He would prop a magazine in front of his face when anyone tried to speak to him or would simply not come out of the bedroom until they left. The one time I invited my coworkers over to our house for an evening, he went to bed immediately and didn't speak to me for three days.

I was not even thirty, and I felt I had nothing to look forward to, nothing to live for. At first I thought that was just part of being "grown up," but I gradually started to wonder if something was wrong. I had given Andrei control of everything—my money, mind, and body—and he had thoroughly and systematically restricted my relationships, my mobility, my future, my whole life. But though I was constantly faced with his rigid opinions about everything from music to money—and his silent-fury way of enforcing them—leaving him never crossed my mind. He was my first serious relationship, and I had never learned to initiate a confrontation or wade through a difficult, emotional conversation with anyone. Ever.

I became increasingly unable to hold up under the isolation, but I didn't know how or what to do differently.

Things went dramatically downhill from there.

25

"Meliss, do you have a minute?"

The phone call comes completely out of the blue, but I always have a minute for my father: the man I adore more than anyone in the world, the person I always wanted to be. I still see him as the *Oxford English Dictionary* and the *Encyclopedia Britannica* combined, wrapped in a multilingual, humorous, bouncy package with sparkling blue eyes and my own winging eyebrows. I worship his every brainwave.

Andrei and I have been married for two years, together for nearly a decade now. We are still attached at the hip, having just finished a marathon training run together, and I am starving and sticky with perspiration. But I stop preparing a box of macaroni and cheese and perch on a dainty, uncomfortable antique chair in the corner of the kitchen we have rebuilt tile by tile.

My father begins to talk.

My mother can call four times per day just to describe her new dish towels, but my father never calls just to talk. This is important, like the time he called to say my Adventist aunt and psychiatrist uncle were getting divorced after twenty years of marriage because Uncle Steve was afraid of bodily fluids and they had never once had sex and my aunt had finally had an affair.

Something like that.

But I never expect what's coming.

As he begins to speak, I stare into the faceted mirror on the wall. My father's distinctive low, crackling voice rumbles like a broken wagon through the blank sweep of my mind, creaking uneasily, pitching out unwanted contents at every lurch. My stomach churns with each sentence, and I wonder if it is post-run starvation or if I am really going to retch, my stomach crawling up through my esophagus to disgorge phantom contents.

Even in a mute shock, I can see gaping holes in his story, inconsistencies streaming through like sunbeams, the whole delicate cloud destined to burn off in the glare of any serious inquiry. I should summon the nerve, be brave enough to ask questions, to get to the truth right now. But his words pile up like merchandise on a conveyor belt, spilling off the sides and into my basket pell-mell without a check as I sit, silent and still.

The story is short, awful, and mercifully vague: he had had an "inappropriate relationship" with a minor when he was an Adventist youth pastor, right around the time I was born. Exactly around the time I was born. They never had sex, he says. But they did everything else.

How Marriage & Family of you, I think.

The now-grown woman recently learned that Dad is shepherding an Adventist church again—he's taken a head pastor position at a Sacramento church after retiring from medicine—and she's requested that the Adventist brass remove him from a position of authority. She believes he is a danger to children.

I look back at the mirror, leaning slowly, deliberately toward the faceted edge until my image explodes into a million slivered shards of angled bits. I stare, unblinking, into the one Picasso'd single-eyeball slice. I cannot breathe.

Dad winds down into embarrassed quiet. Neither he nor I know how to hang up.

I stretch one leg that has cramped into an insensate claw beneath me, needles of pain leaping up through my thigh. "Well, you know," I say gamely after an interminable silence, "if we were all bound by the mistakes we made when we were twenty-five, we'd never succeed in life." I am all of twenty-eight, but only someone who feels like they are sixty could say a thing like this.

The acute embarrassment on the other end of the line deepens. Maybe he doesn't want to think that I too have had indiscretions, let alone what they might be. Maybe one mind-blowing confession per family is all that's allowed.

I don't know how to make my father feel better, how to shove him back up on Mount Olympus. Perhaps if he had been an alcoholic instead of a charming, wide-eyed intellectual, I would have been prepared by years of drunken rages or fits of depression to step in as the caretaker, but I am not equipped now for this role reversal. I don't know how to ease a parent's guilty conscience. Ours has been a completely scandal-free family, or so it had seemed.

I don't remember now how the conversation ended. I wish I could, because somehow that seems important. I do know that after we hung up, my father called my sister and told her an abbreviated versions of the same story. For some reason I was gifted with the long version, the widescreen edition, the first run. I found it odd and uncomfortable that somehow I had gotten more detail than my sister. Perhaps he had meant it as a personal, reassuring touch since I was our family's token "feminist" and it concerned a crime against women.

Of course, no one is calling it a crime at the time, especially not me. I didn't call it a crime until years later, when I found the victim.

26

After I hung up, I sat for what must have been hours. Like salt on a slug, the conversation dissolved so much of what I thought my life was right before my eyes. Everything I had known twisted and foamed, shriveled into a revolting, slimy mess. I did not know what to think or to do, but the news did shift something in me. I knew one thing I could *not* do anymore: I could not have sex with Andrei ever again.

Over time the sex had slowly gone from violently scary to super cringey daddy-daughter role play. The daddy game was a constant, and it shared the bed with Andrei's other fantasies, role plays that routinely turned me into something—just about anything—other than myself. By the time we finally went to that therapist, the one with the smoker's voice and annoying questions about why I thought sex had to be bad, I wasn't only sick of being some*one* else; I desperately wanted to be some*where* else.

When therapy didn't help, we made a last-ditch effort to rehabilitate our union by packing up our fragile marriage, our sexual standoff, and taking an Italian vacation. We had been planning it for years, and neither of us was the type to give up; it seemed more imaginable that our union would fail than that we wouldn't go through with something we'd spent money on. In Rome, in a room with mosquito blood on the walls and a spectacular view of the Trevi Fountain, I offered a blow job to diffuse the tension.

We were leaning out the window, glasses of red wine in hand, watching a Japanese wedding photo shoot below. I had read somewhere that destination weddings were all the rage in Japan. In my ear Andrei kept up a continuous whine, channeling the mosquitoes before the stolen tourist blood became a fresco on the wallpaper. Rubbing against me, groping and insisting, he bullied and pleaded for sex.

It was a weird time and place to stake my first "no." Big fat tears, hot and salty as antipasti, slid quietly down my face as I gazed at Triton blowing his horn. Were any of the tourists glancing up wondering what the girl with the view had to cry about?

I turned from the window, angry and trapped and thinking it was simply easier to give in. I offered Andrei conciliatory oral sex, a Hail Mary blow job in the eleventh hour. After six months of celibacy, it felt awkward and forced. The silence was deafening.

Was this what she did with my father?

I gagged. I retired with the taste of defeat in my mouth.

Even though we passed it at least six times a day, Andrei never threw a coin over his shoulder into the Trevi like all the other tourists who hoped it would guarantee they'd come back again. Apparently he did not want to return to Rome. I, on the other hand, never wanted to leave the Eternal City with its famous excess of fountains. With their purifying streams of water endlessly washing the writhing, sexually charged stone hedonists portrayed in them, those fountains reminded me in a perverse way of my baptism.

My father had performed my baptism in a special Sabbath afternoon ceremony. He was special to the church, of course—a revered preacher physician—so I got special treatment. All Seventh-day Adventists are fully immersed at baptism near the age of twelve, when they are supposedly old enough to decide for themselves whether or not to accept the religion. Not surprisingly, I did not give any thought to religious devotion, but I was all for being in the spotlight.

My father stepped into the tank before me, the white robe momentarily floating up around his waist and drifting on the surface of the water like a discarded trash bag. I caught a mortifying glimpse of his underwear before the robe sank limply to cling to his legs. When it was my turn to enter the water, I carefully held my robe down at my sides, preventing any trash-bag mermaid moments of my own. My father held a cloth in his left hand to cover my face while dunking me. I took my place in front of him, holding onto his left wrist and staring at the little pad of gauze. I wondered if my mascara would run.

He raised his right hand high above me and went through a speech about my grown-up, adult choice to officially join the church and devote myself to God. If I had wanted to eat meat or swim on a Saturday, the religious leaders would never have allowed me to make that choice, but for this single moment in seventh grade I unwittingly played out their farce of autonomy, just long enough to dedicate myself to the church forever.

The baptismal speech concluded with a series of questions and answers, like the vows in a wedding. I do take this religion and this God to be my master; I promise to love and obey. My father asked the questions, and I answered them. In the end, instead of a kiss or a ring, I was dedicated to the Father, Son, and Holy Spirit, and I was plunged beneath the font.

Two hours of hot rollers, hairspray, and makeup gone in an instant.

I never thought of my baptism again until I was trapped in Rome with an estranged husband and more fountains than any city in the world. I mused on the corrosive nature of the continual rinsing of those ancient statues, their twisted heathen bodies perpetually washed clean of their sins by the Eternal City's water. Instead of purifying the participants or their acts, these baptisms wore away the fragile bodies beneath them with acidic, polluted repetition.

Later in Florence, where I tried one final time to have sex with Andrei, I bought red lipstick, beautiful strappy heels, and a pleated leather purse shaped like a bowling ball. I stared at the David's beautiful hands for hours, trying to imagine a fulfilling sexual relationship, trying to picture what "good" sex was. But nothing could get me in the mood to have sex with my husband ever again.

We couldn't do it. *I* couldn't do it. I hated him.

A simple explanation was that I hated him because I couldn't hate my father. I was still decades from understanding what patriarchy was and how it had owned me since birth—how particular awful family dynamics had maimed and stunted everything about my life. So I went with the simple explanation.

After the bombshell phone call, no one in my family was willing to discuss the facts or fallout from my father's past, leaving me very unclear about the extent of his crimes. Dad treated it as a minor incident, and Mom bounced between cryptic, angry statements and blithe denial. After living at home until age thirty and struggling to establish autonomy and independence, my sister was finally on a streak of incredible freedom and growth, and her fragile self-reliance was too hard-won to risk venturing back into painful family territory. I figured it was up to me to get to the bottom of it all. I was owed the truth, whatever that might be, and anyway, I had always been the problem child, the strong-willed child.

The next time my parents came into town to visit me, I asked them to lunch—an entirely awkward and formal thing to do in our family. There at my favorite Mexican restaurant, I confronted them over the chip basket. I demanded to know if they were holding back any more secrets.

Whereupon Mom blurted out that she must protect her family's money from the lawsuits of the preteen "street urchins" who had seduced her poor husband so long ago.

Just like that, I learned there was more than one.

Of course there were.

When I asked how old these women had been, my dad just blinked, sad and owl-eyed, immobilized by direct confrontation. My mother shrugged dismissively and said, "Young, very young," but claimed not to remember names or ages. They both insisted there was nothing left to tell, that I now knew all.

We never discussed it again.

Dad apparently made some sort of public confession at the church where he was head pastor and resigned. For a while my mother threatened to divorce him to protect her money from potential lawsuits. I did not know what was going to happen, who actually knew what, or how much there truly was to know. The only clear thing was that my parents needed to move out of the church-provided housing quickly.

I pictured my parents leaving their apartment in separate moving vans in the event Mom made good on her divorce threats: one van for her, filled with box after box of carefully labeled china—"Depression glass vases," "gold Havilland serving dishes," "Grandma Sarah's porcelain"—stacked next to mountains of heavy antique furniture and bins of creamy Eastern European linens; the other van for my father, packed deep with unmarked book boxes. There would have been no need to label them; he would have sat for days on each end of the trip sorting through his favorite companions, reorganizing and rereading piles and piles of well-thumbed volumes.

Where would they go? How would they survive separated, alone? My father never could cook. My mother couldn't stand to be by herself. Would Dad become one of those little bent-over men sitting solo at a diner counter? Would Mom continue to collect sets of china to place around an empty grand table every Saturday after church, holding court when no one came?

We had moved so many times during my childhood, the whole thing was a blur, but if there was one thing I was good at, it was packing books and china. No one asked for my help, but I wanted to get away from my marriage, so I volunteered to assist my parents in packing up and skulking out of their community. I couldn't imagine many of their church members would be clamoring to lend a hand at that point, if Dad indeed had done as he claimed and "told them everything."

Mom had retracted or forgotten her passing threat of divorce by the time I called to say I was coming, firmly commanding me to forget about my father's whole story when I ventured to ask. She declared it all "just one sin" equal to any other, just like not quite waiting for the sun to set on Saturday so that we could go swimming as kids. And, after all, the Church and Ellen White had always put forth that men's adultery is entirely women's fault, so Mom grimly insisted that her husband's indiscretion was simply the "cross God gives women to bear."

I made the several-hour trek from where I still resided with Andrei in LA to my parents' house, one depressing, dysfunctional dynamic as good as another.

27

My parents don't have friends and they don't have dinner parties, so Mom has always used church as an excuse to invite near strangers over for elaborately set, blandly cooked meals on Saturday afternoons. Thanks to many mission trips to China, Mexico, Belarus, Ukraine, and all the other places the Adventist Church dangled medical care and English lessons in exchange for church membership, Mom and Dad have always been guaranteed a nearly endless stream of newly converted immigrants to stun with eighteen-place table settings and unidentifiable entrees.

Sabbath lunch is nearly always the same feast, served summer and winter on a bewildering array of formal table settings: cucumber slices drowning in lemon and radioactive-orange Lawry's salt, vegetarian stroganoff, a slimy, sweet mixture of ketchup, sour cream, and cream of mushroom soup that is always curdled and served over rice, and root beer floats. My maternal grandparents had a full diner-style soda fountain bar in their Southern California house from which my teenaged mother served her friends vanilla ice cream drowning in root beer. The soda fountain had long been defunct, the lidded containers for maraschino cherries and nuts becoming playthings for grandchildren, but the classic '50s drink has obviously remained a symbol of fun and hospitality to Mom, even when we lived in Michigan with its subzero temperatures.

Everything else, from broccoli to Special K loaf, is always cooked to the consistency of mashed potatoes in what I assume is an effort to protect the china. Even standard dinner knife blades can wreak havoc on bone china and gold filigree—just one note in the thousands of helpful things I know about tableware. To accompany the meal, Mom has enough glassware to stock an entire winery. Her table invariably sparkles with so much crystal it looks like a chandelier has leapt to its death, but Adventists don't drink, so she never serves alcohol. Instead, she tends her stash of sparkling juices like a seasoned oenophile, chortling over each Martinelli's blend: "Which one is this? Oh! It's apple *raspberry*!" Each place setting boasts several different goblets to receive the prized array of "frizzle" while martini glasses hold Jell-O studded with shredded carrots and raisins and high balls contain the revered root beer floats.

My mother is not in the least unusual in her bland and pedestrian style of cooking; Adventist fine cuisine is an oxymoron, their potluck meals remaining virtually unchanged since the 1950s: scalloped potatoes, green bean casserole topped with mushroom soup and onion crisps, and lots of unnaturally colored Jell-O salad full of nuts and marshmallows. And let's not forget the many versions of that Special K loaf, a meatloaf substitute made with the wheat flakes created by John Harvey Kellogg while promoting his so-called high fiber cereals as the best way to control unholy urges and lust. That, combined with yogurt enemas and circumcision, was apparently his go-to sin saver, but thank God nobody discusses those at potluck.

In spite of the effort she puts into her table settings, meals at Mom's are not meant to be the long, drool-worthy feasts of deep conversation and lively debate that I experienced during college when I ran off to France for the summer. There guests would get into heated arguments over tables groaning with food that it took all day to plan and prepare, and just in case conversation lagged and needed a jumpstart, the centerpiece was once an orgy of naked Barbies in lewd positions nestled amongst potted flowers.

By contrast, formal Adventist meals are the hair shirt of eating, like every other SDA custom: a sober, slightly painful act of dedication, with no invigorating mental fodder, no interesting gastronomic intake, no stimulation of any kind. Eat quickly and solemnly and stay in your lane, and at my mother's table, be sure to talk about the table settings.

There will be no more lavish church lunches for Mom now, though.

When Dad originally took the retirement job as pastor and they moved to California's capital city, my mother somehow convinced her gay Adventist landlord to revamp the apartment to her specifications. A significant proportion of my father's church was composed of gay and lesbian members, and he was so proud of the fact that Adventist doctrine "did not ask homosexuals to change their orientation." They were simply forbidden "to practice" their evil ways. The irony of Dad's sin having been overlooked for his decades of church celebrity while theirs was demonized never seems to have registered with anyone. I imagine the lonely landlord bonding with my mother, finding emotional solace and the love otherwise denied them both by idiotic and hurtful church mandates in a riotous celebration of paint colors and dish patterns.

I walk upstairs, where there are half-packed boxes everywhere. The space is a miniature of every house we have ever lived in: high ceilings, dark Victorian woodwork, heavy tapestries, and velvet curtains festooned with an astonishing array of gold tassels and cords, antiques from a bewildering collection of eras set against brooding burgundy and blue walls. "We girls do this so well, don't we?" Mom giggles, settling in to fill quilted zipper bags with stacks of plates, placing a slice of foam between each one. "I haven't broken a single dish in all these moves, not even when we had to move across country twice. Though we lost a box once and the shipping company returned it destroyed!"

I hand Mom a pair of scissors as she deftly seals the package and assembles a new one.

"Do you remember the pink and gray rose china that was one of my wedding presents? They really did a number on it. But even then some pieces came through just fine because I had wrapped them so well!" She reaches for the next item without taking a breath, the slightest grimace flickering for a moment. "I never did like those dishes, so I didn't care."

There is a brief pause as she stands to reach a delicate tower of teacups on the shelf above her head. Balancing tableware is just about the only activity that requires such total focus that she cannot distract herself with chatter. Then—"Oh, look!" She picks at a yellowing booklet curled in the lid of a gold-rimmed teapot and tosses it to me. "That was the program from when your father was ordained." Grabbing a huge bag of Styrofoam peanuts, she rips into it, causing it to explode all over our neatly organized china skyscrapers. Peaks of teapots and casserole lids rise out of the messy white fluff like the tops of the Bay Bridge in a deep fog.

I look carefully at the booklet, a program from the Adventist pastor ordination ceremony of 1971. It is folded to the page containing a biography of my father under a picture of the four of us: my sparkly-eyed, Brando father; my gorgeous, deer-in-the-headlights mother, coiffed with a big beehive; my wide-eyed four-year-old sister in curled pigtails and a sheer Barbara-Streisand-at-the-Oscars pantsuit; and one-year-old me, mouth agog, with a multilayered crocheted dress and velvet bow clearly intended to countermand my androgynous baby look. While I stare at the picture, my mother furiously shoves Styrofoam into the bottom of the next box. I try to sit as still and silent as a birdwatcher so as not to scare her off.

"Mom?" I say quietly. "This program is from 1971. That's after I was born." I press on before she can send the insensible word barrage to dig a moat. "The church made Dad an official pastor *after* I was born? They ordained him, even after he . . ." I stumble, groping for the right words. "*After* what he did . . . ?"

"Did you see the bow I put in your hair?" my mother interrupts. "I had the hardest time getting it to stay in your hair, you know, you've always had the finest, softest hair! I think I cried, I really cried—I *did!*—trying to get that bow to stay, and it was still crooked!" She slams the lid onto the teapot, twisting paper around the bulbous shape a couple of times and placing it quickly in the box. "And do you remember that outfit Sophia was wearing? It had lace around the ankles—they were bell bottoms, I think, do you remember them?"

Yes. I got to wear them after she did. I remember.

Je me reviens.

I watch my twitchy, manic mother—all traces of beauty long buried under a habitual, tight-lipped frown—and I mourn the toll her beliefs have taken. I also congratulate myself on being so free of them. I would never let the Church and God and men ruin my life like that. I have escaped.

"Mom, can I have some juice?" I ask.

She brightens immediately. As she bustles off to decant her finest and put it in a goblet, I take one more look at the beautiful young mother with two toddlers, living in the dusty farmlands of California with a child-molesting, God-blessed intellectual. Then I take the teapot out and carefully repack it, tucking the picture back in under the lid.

We go on with our picture-perfect family, all surface love and buried secrets. My parents do not divorce as they move on to their next home, their next life. But I do.

28

My marriage to Andrei died precisely as it had begun: on a cold and rainy morning. I left him standing motionless in our living room swaddled in a fluffy, white bathrobe—a padded, emasculating version of the martial arts uniform that had so seduced me on first sight years earlier. His face was swollen and tear-streaked. I appeared to have broken my husband.

I was closing the door on one man with another firmly in my sights, as would become my pattern—and he was already in more than just my sights. It was the late '90s heyday of tech startups, and businesses had spilled over from downtown Los Angeles to all the nearby beach towns such as the one where Andrei and I resided. There had been multiple stabs at rebranding various areas "Silicon Beach" and filling the inveterate surf towns with "laid-back tech culture" companies, but these were all fairly ill-advised and short-lived. Nobody really wanted to work at the beach; they only wanted to build a home and hang out there. So the high-tech high was more of a whippet than a bender, and the towns all soon went back to what they did best: white liberal self-importance and exorbitantly overpriced housing.

But for a time there was a start-up on every corner from Long Beach to Malibu, and during the initial frenzy, about a year before Dad's announcement and the implosion of my marriage, I scored a job with one of the promising new companies. I began as a receptionist with the agreement that I would move into a technical writing position whenever one opened up. It had been Andrei's idea, a smart one, as were nearly all of his business assessments. The company he pushed me toward was instrumental in the birth of camera-phone sharing and social media, and for a while our company doubled in size nearly every six months. I only briefly served at the front desk before my promotion to the writing department, and I was drafting copy for photo-sharing website prototypes before my first Christmas with the company.

As our product heated up and my hours got longer and longer, Andrei's death grip on my schedule and whereabouts necessarily began to loosen a bit. He still dropped me off at work, picked me up afterwards, and controlled all our outside activities, but we both worked extraordinarily long start-up workdays, and eventually I had to get my own method of transportation: a cute Honda scooter. With my own wheels and within the safe walls of my company, I began to blossom a bit.

A large part of every employee's job during our marathon weeks was constantly testing our top-secret technology. Every Monday morning we all traipsed into the office tasked with sharing and resharing, looking and liking, editing and commenting on photos displayed on the latest build by the programmers. And all week, every week, our entire user interface team was treated to endless, captivating photo collections of my coworker, Todd, and his magical family and fathering duties. It was one long Technicolor parade of blue eyes and blue skies, a Hallmark slideshow of love, laughter, and light spirits. Backyard barbeques, late-night bonfires, and fireworks. Beach trips, biking, camping, fishing, face painting, jaunts to the San Bernardino Mountains to frolic in the snow. Even yard cleanup looked amazing with his two gorgeous children.

Todd himself was the absolute embodiment of fun. Soft-spoken but high-spirited and never without an impish grin, he was always up for a good time and absolutely adored by everyone in the office. He was also levelheaded, kind, and good-looking, seemingly the most wonderful and devoted dad, husband, and all-around family man I had ever seen. He would meet his wife and kids for lunch; he would duck out of our marathon work sessions faithfully to pick the children up from daycare. He would speak glowingly, at length, about his baby girl's birth or his red-eye mornings of cupcakes and cartoons with his toddler son. He was rabidly, ecstatically involved in every aspect of parenting, as far as I could tell, something I found incredibly charming.

I had personally always firmly dismissed the idea of having children; my own parents and religious upbringing had rendered the idea of motherhood the antithesis of appealing, and once I was drowning in Andrei's all-consuming, ironfisted demands, I had doubled down on my childbearing ban. I instinctively, vehemently refused to expand the list of people entitled to my life; his possessive suffocation was more than enough. Children surely would be the cinderblock to irrevocably sink me in the dark swamp of a tiny, dull life.

But Todd made parenthood look like the most exclusive, intoxicating party ever.

We began to hang out together during software builds—a process that would sometimes take hours before a fresh version was stable enough to test—and the endless late-night QA-testing-and-release sessions slowly turned into confessional drinking fests. As Todd described his crazy twenties in college, I began to realize how thoroughly I had been robbed of my twenties and early thirties by a prematurely middle-aged man whose primary interest in me seemed to have been to hide me away from the world.

Todd was everything my husband was not: a sweet, social, happy, warm man. Gregarious and athletic, he radiated a steady, uncomplicated normalcy that I had never in my life felt, a magnetic, palpable calm and ease so radically different from the tense, unspoken undercurrent vibrating throughout my upbringing and experience. He was also one of the first people I knew completely devoid of the sneering superiority I had been raised with, projecting a genuinely curious and caring attitude toward all human beings that I still admire and struggle to emulate.

And his family was so unlike mine. They all socialized often and boisterously, genuinely appreciated and respected each other, and were consistently low conflict. They did normal things, had no apparent drama, laughed often, judged rarely. Todd seemed to have never suffered large-scale tragedies, assaults, or injustices in life. Everyone loved him, and I soaked up the happy simplicity of being around him. And I definitely relished the opportunity to carouse with him. Easy nights as drinking buddies morphed into becoming good friends, and soon we had fallen hard and fast, messily overlapping our doomed marriages with an intense new relationship.

Our open-secret burgeoning love had barely ignited when my biological clock kicked into warp speed. To my complete shock at thirty-two, as I contemplated some sort of normal life for the first time ever, the baby-craving glockenspiel began to spin around me, taunting me with burbling cherubs at every turn. The world was full of babies, and I needed one desperately. I could feel it in my bones, in my womb. It suddenly seemed so clear that having children did not have to be yet another deadweight in a joyless future of servitude. Todd was obviously proof of that: family, all kinds of family, could be fun. Who knew?

I started researching sperm banks and half-heartedly contemplated solo parenthood, tentatively asking Todd if he wanted to just procreate with me and stay casual. But he couldn't see his way to anything so unconventional—if we were going to have children, we were going to be married—and to be fair, I couldn't quite picture being that unconventional either. Within a couple of years of meeting, we had each divorced, and our relationship had fast-tracked into engagement and marriage. I was pregnant a couple months after the wedding, and we had a child before our first anniversary.

Unfortunately, my beautiful firstborn arrived early in a blockbuster powder ski season. During the first four months of our son's existence, my husband was home for exactly three weekends, leaving me alone for the other twelve with a sleepless newborn—and sometimes his other children as well—while he frolicked on the white-blanketed slopes of the nearest ski resorts. That year was followed by a similar one, and another baby. Overnight I went from happy new bride to lonely, semi-single mother in a small and crowded cement house, raising two babies, two young stepchildren, and a dog I had specified I did not want.

It was a shocking revelation, coming as quickly as it did: my adorable, gadabout husband—though the absolute picture of financial responsibility, easy temperament, and cheerful normalcy—had sweetly participated in my wish to bear offspring but did not appear to really want the strenuous grind of round-the-clock tending to babies and young children. He had already been there, done that.

And it was no simple two-person union we were attempting, either. We had plunged impulsively, optimistically into a very complicated sprawl of relationships: a stepfamily, back-to-back babies, ex-spouses, and his lovely but omnipresent parents who visited and stayed in the living room of our tiny house for weeks at a time. It quickly became clear that, even with great love and the best intentions, we had each come to the partnership with deeply flawed assumptions and goals that neither was able to articulate or willing to give up, and on which we would instead double down as the years progressed.

29

It's Baby Jesus's birthday and my husband left me yesterday and I am sitting on an empty plane alone, trapped in a tin can in the air, suspended over somewhere, anchored nowhere.

It's not really the Christ child's birthday, of course, this made-up pagan holiday lionized by Christians in one of their earliest cultural appropriation exercises. And my husband didn't really leave me for good, he just left me in the airport with our infant and injured toddler on Christmas Eve so that he could continue with his other children on the family Christmas trip while I handle a hospital visit.

And I'm not really alone—I am the customary sole caretaker of that infant and that toddler. We are the round-two knockoffs, my babies and I, repeated absences and desertions such as today's pasted on us like sale stickers, the marks of our devaluation. By this point we seem to have hit the clearance table.

I guess it is blasphemous to say such things, to say all the quiet parts out loud, though my thoughts right now make me distinctly less happy than blaspheming usually does. I am not even remotely happy. I am incredibly sad and alone. I am this way a lot.

My cranky infant is in a sling on my chest because she's teething and it soothes her to be near my heartbeat, as erratic as it currently is. My toddler sits at my feet wearing a sling of his own, the strap around his little neck immobilizing his arm because I gave him Nursemaid's Elbow—dislocated it in a rage in the airport security line because he was throwing a fit on the floor and would not get up. We had been trying to get four children under twelve through security, and I was secretly dreading the week ahead—full of everyone having great fun while I ran the endless cycle of putting children down for naps and bedtime alone—and I yanked too hard to get my melting-down toddler up off the floor.

I took him straight to the emergency room after my husband left for happier climes, and they popped the joint back in place in a practiced, lightning-fast move while simultaneously giving him a teddy bear. The doctor reassured me that this was a very common accidental injury, no need to involve CPS. I had not even considered that option—that anyone could think I had intentionally endangered or injured my own child—but it has taken over my brain ever since, a swelling, paralyzing, encephalitic shame and self-hatred: you're a terrible mother, an awful human being, full of all those unallowable, unnamed *bad* feelings.

The doctor said my child doesn't need the sling but gave it to us anyway for comfort, and I want him to have it—he seems to like it, and it is the least that I can do, to honor the fact that I hurt him. I also need him to have the sling to remind me that I am a worthless and horrible person, to rub the salt in my own wounds, to parade myself in chains in public. I have become the thing I feared most in life; I have become my own mother: a perpetually angry woman, volatile, brittle, brutal, bitter, taking out her marital fears and frustrations in furious bursts on her own children.

I feel none of those bad things right now, though. I feel other, equally unacknowledgeable ones: I am very, very sad and scared.

I have suffered from a terrible fear of flying most of my adult life, a full-blown phobia on a completely debilitating scale. I am not just an anxious flyer. I am a Marge-Simpson-level, screaming-and-running-up-and-down-the-aisle flyer. But of course I would never, *ever* make a public spectacle like that, *actually* screaming and running, so my body deals with the floods of panic silently, without my consent. I faint. I black out. I lose control of my bowels.

After years of trying and failing with everything from hypnosis to cognitive therapy to silly classes with "graduation flights" that condescendingly hand you the statistics of how safe flying is—as if panic listens to statistics—I eventually found something that got me through air travel relatively well: a mixture of valium and alcohol. I have to monitor the mix carefully, adjusting constantly to account for extra turbulence and length of flight. It is a precarious balance of topping off or backing off in order to maintain a semi-functional numbness while my panicking body runs through the substances at an astounding yet always unpredictable rate.

My husband knows this process quite well since we have traveled together often over the years, but he left his two tiny and incredibly helpless children with me anyway so that he and his older children won't miss the family holiday celebration across the country. He made a half-hearted offer to stay, but mostly he insisted we just throw the injured kid on the plane and "he'll get over it," as if it were all simply drama inconveniencing the Christmas plans. Extended family awaited us, and we all knew it would be doubly my fault if I ruined everything by asking him and his older kids not to get on the plane.

I never even consider asking my husband to stay, never think to expect the father of my children to help them and help me. I do not expect support and sacrifice from men. Instead, I slowly maneuver the children back through security solo, somehow navigating to the hospital with my luggage, the diaper bag, an infant strapped to my chest, and a toddler. I had to do it all again in the morning, in reverse, still just me and the babies.

I take the kids home after the hospital for a few hours' sleep, get up, and do just that: drive back to the airport, security, luggage, infant, diaper bag, toddler in a sling. There is no option to opt out; our presence is expected and we had to fly out first thing, even though it's Christmas Day. My mother-in-law has scheduled family pictures to be taken after Christmas, so our total absence would ruin everything even more than I already have.

Finally safely on the plane, I ponder: is anyone wondering how we are doing? Is my husband wishing he had stayed to support his son through his first serious injury and hospital visit? Is he worried that I will dope up as usual, a carefully titrated zombie focused on one simple task at a time, barely able to maintain my own basic consciousness and only fuzzily aware that I have small children to care for? Or does he assume I will go cold sober and risk absolute panic the entire time, perhaps fainting, perhaps losing control, perhaps traumatizing the children with some bizarre bodily failure? Does he wonder what will happen to our two-under-three if I pass out and do not come to?

Is anyone thinking of us at all?

I have no way of knowing. They are celebrating Christmas today, and we are flying.

Somehow, some way or other, I do manage to more or less calmly get my two tiny dependents through an extended day of multiple flights from coast to coast drug-free, both sober and without embarrassing incidents. The adrenaline drowns out any actual memories of the trip, my only recollection being how often kindly flight attendants and pilots wish us a Merry Christmas on mostly empty planes and how much it hurts every time.

We finally arrive on the East Coast well after dark, exhausted, strung out, rumpled. We are greeted by a giddily happy extended family, bellies full and ready for bed after a long celebratory day, everyone cozy in their Christmas gift pajamas. Tomorrow we will all dress in coordinated outfits to indicate we are one big, happy family, but tonight there is no mistaking that my children and I are the odd ones out.

There are light jokes made about me as a child abuser. No jokes about an absentee husband and father. I grit my teeth and smile, my jaw already sore from its terror-clench all day. The jokes sting, of course, and I wonder what has been said in my absence today. I wonder what they all really thought of me while I was in the sky, up and down, up and down, struggling across the entire country toting little children and diaper bags and broken dreams by myself.

Everyone trickles again into the darkened formal dining room, gathering around us under the twinkling lights of the enormous, meticulously decorated tree. There are a few scattered presents still under it, forlorn and upended in a mostly empty space, resembling nothing more than the jumbled bargain table at the end of a last-call sale.

These are our presents. And here we are. The after-Christmas sale items have arrived.

Instead of trying to fix our marriage, Todd and I loyally soldiered onward, drifting further and further into our own worlds. Todd worked long, hard hours and socialized longer and harder. I grew angrier and more bitter, trying to redeem myself with my only coping mechanism: perfectionism and control. I drove for every field trip, wrote articles to publicize Todd's brilliant sports equipment design hobby, dumped my own cash into an RV and then a vacation house so that we could go to the snow every weekend as a family (even though I despised camping and snow sports). I hosted Todd's sports crew after their weekly outings, socialized with his friends, ferried the older children to tae kwon do and summer school. I took all the kids on summer trips with me to lake houses and wine country relatives, and I led "Melissa Camp" for them in the summer. When it seemed likely that we would eventually take over his family's ancestral East Coast property, I threw myself into the study of all things Early American. I joined the Junior League (the women's leadership training organization); I set up a foundation website for the estate, I stockpiled research on how to maintain historic properties, and I began a mailing list for future donors.

No matter how doggedly I tried to hammer myself into a bland, brain-lite Stepford wife, however, and no matter how gamely Todd kept at his lucrative but creatively unfulfilling job, our core conflicts remained. They widened. I think both of us felt trapped, abandoned, and deeply unhappy, but we could not voice our resentment in productive ways. I didn't have the relationship skills; I didn't have the models. Most importantly, I didn't have the awareness that I deserved to ask for better. The only approved skill sets and coping mechanisms I had been given were to be pleasing, to be submissive and pretty and to suppress and deny any bad feelings. If that all failed, it was my fault—so bring on the binging and purging, the self-denigration and immolation in sexual sacrifice.

But none of those former coping mechanisms worked in my current marital situation, leaving me at a complete loss. Equally unable to parse our basic problems, Todd just tried to walk the tightrope of my dissatisfaction or, more often, disappeared to party elsewhere—going on ski weekends and bike tours and dancing at Lady Gaga concerts and sucking down beers balanced on the heads of full-busted frauleins at local Oktoberfest blowouts—things that I often only learned about months or even years later from other people's party pictures or from my children. All I could do was seethe and sulk, directing my impotent anger at everything from his dog to my own children, crushing everything down inside myself until it exploded in venomous, sarcastic, personal attacks in late-night battles with my husband. There I would drunkenly unload scathing ripostes on adjacent people, behaviors, and situations that were symptoms or side effects, but I never adequately addressed the underlying structural issues.

The best I could do was dig deeper into motherhood. I tried to raise the perfect children, throwing my miserably unwilling toddlers into tennis and swimming, language lessons, and Montessori preschools, flooding them with foreign language books and expensive mail-order cartoons in German and French. My perfectionism was anything but perfect. My housekeeping was nonexistent, my personal maintenance minimal. I was angry and lonely and empty.

And yet my lifelong quest for that miserable perfection brought about the most unexpected reward.

30

As my oldest child approaches preschool age, I obsessively google ratings for all public and private schools in California. Scrolling away, I am suddenly accosted by an article about the Monterey Bay Academy.

I have entirely blocked out the fact that Central California hosts both the biggest Adventist Camp Meeting and a very swaggy boarding school, the posh, beach cliff setting through which my rich cousins once swanned. I begged to attend as a twelve-year-old, pining to escape the dowdy bowels of the Midwest for the glamor of the liberal "Left Coast" Adventists, but of course my requests went unheeded.

I click on the article.

Lurid droplets of scandal instantly draw me in, and I read, riveted, sneer-scrolling, a tale of horrific sex abuse at MBA in the mid-1980s. I wonder idly if one of my cousins, who attended at that approximate time, can give me the real dirt. In the article there are only the usual denials—"the Adventist Church has a zero-tolerance policy for abuse of any kind"—and then a few accounts of other SDA sex abuse cases from all over the United States. In one interview, an extremely angry and articulate older woman, a research scientist, details her abuse at the hands of a youth pastor in the '60s in California.

My body absorbs this before my mind makes the connection. My finger clamps rigidly on the mouse, and I begin to shake, causing the screen to fly by. Picking the claw hand up with my other, I tap the arrow key painstakingly to scroll back, reading in reverse, as if that will change anything.

She is talking about my father.

And there is a name. The reality of that name—a fairly ordinary one—rips into me. *Dr. Z.*

Who *are* you, Dr. Z?

Maybe you can help? Can you tell me what to really think about my father? What to think about my entire life? Did Dad feel guilt—was he remorseful? Or did he think he was above the rules he expounded from the pulpit and enforced in his own home? What did the Church do? What did my mother say? How old were you? How many other girls were there? How did it end?

Are you okay?

I print the article out, instinctively afraid somehow it will disappear into pixels and vapor and I will never find it or her again.

But I don't know if I want to find her again. I don't know if I want to see her or hear her or read her.

I bury the clipping in a file where it gathers dust in a box in the back of a closet. I try to forget about it for months on end. I can't bring myself to throw it out, yet keeping it seems dangerous, like a Trojan horse; this gift from my random googling might disgorge an army of destruction inside of me and my family if I truly let it in.

I am not wrong.

I cannot forget the article. I remember it every time I look at my youngest child, a girl. I relive the fear that hit me in the delivery room when it was announced that I had brought a female into the world. Dragging with her out of my womb, an awful ancestral placenta, came the nameless terror mothers everywhere feel over the dangerous uncertainties our girls will inevitably face.

Now I know that was exactly how my mother must have felt the day I was born.

I dig out the clipping.

I find Dr. Z's name and address in the large city she calls home. I write a short note and put it in the mail.

> *Dear Dr. Z,*
>
> *Two years ago I stumbled across a newspaper interview in which you discussed recent abuse cases in the Seventh-day Adventist Church. It has taken me these two years to work up the courage to write to you.*
>
> *. . .*
>
> *There is no reason for you to relive an excruciating period of your life for my benefit, yet I would be so grateful if you could help shed light on this very confusing and painful family issue for me.*
>
> *. . .*
>
> *I have no hope of getting the truth from the church or my family. You are the only person I can turn to.*
> *Melissa S*

I wait for a reply.

I don't know if she will reply.

I don't know if I want a reply.

As time drags on, I figure she doesn't want to hear from me—but then something tells me that isn't true. If she was willing to talk to the newspaper, she was likely ready to talk to me. Maybe she was even looking for me, too.

I google her name again and, for the love of all things unholy, there is another physician in that same city by the same name, and this Dr. Z has a more accurate scientific specialty. I don't know how I mixed them up, how I didn't see them both the first time. To this day there is a woman out there, a kindly doctor, I picture, who received the most random and brutal letter out of the blue, one begging for her assistance in a generations-long family pain cycle that is still a complete mystery to her.

Somehow it seems fitting that my super-secretive family's shame has probably ended up sitting somewhere in someone's desk drawer, a random oddity to be occasionally brought out and pondered. I picture that other doctor, even if she be kindly, pulling it out to read and joke about at dinner parties, a punchline to chuckle over, then dismiss.

I write to the other Dr. Z.

She replies immediately.

31

Opening an email should really be harder. Physical letters offer soothing rituals that prepare the recipient for their contents: Tap tap. Rip rip rip. Extract. Unfold. I can handle this. The tangible act of opening allows me some fleeting, feeble illusion of control over what spills out, no matter how gruesome.

But an electronic inbox is a traumatizing peep show, strutting naked messages exposing themselves at an alarming rate. I have no warning before one of them goes commando in plain view:

> *Dear Melissa,*
> *The last time I saw you, you were a very beautiful newborn! I think I always expected to hear from you at some point.*
>
> *I can only say that I was a very immature little girl who wanted desperately to be part of a family. I was raised by my grandparents after my parents abandoned me, and I got caught up in a situation with your dad that was extremely hurtful.*
>
> *The attached photo is from my 13th birthday party. I was already having a relationship with Paul at the time. I had cut my hair to look as much as possible like your mom, Elizabeth.*

I recoil at her use of my parents' first names. No one ever refers to my father so casually. He has an array of titles and degrees to pick from, after all; how dare she, a mere kid, be on a first-name basis with my father? Of course, Dr. Z is a much titled, much degreed fifty-something herself now and has had some sort of sex with him, so what ceremony is there left to stand on? In fact, what ground am I standing on at all?

Carefully avoiding the embedded picture, I inspect the borders of the email like I do with horror movies: when things get too scary, I concentrate on finding the edges of the screen in the dark, inspecting and defining them against the heavy velvet curtains and letting the violence dance safely around in my peripheral vision. In the header bar her email address catches my attention. It features the name of a king of Assyria who mounted an aggressive military expansion campaign in the first century BCE, plundering Israel and Judah among other conquests. It is the kind of name only my father would have bandied about.

> *I had a typical schoolgirl crush on him because he made me feel so special. All of my girlfriends did too. I seemed to be the one he singled out though. He drew little hearts on my schoolwork with yellow chalk when he was teaching us Bible. He taught me to drive the stick shift in his old VW Bug by holding his hand over mine while shifting gears.*

I loved our faded blue VW Bug because I was almost born in the passenger seat. Dr. Z's driving lessons took place mere months before my parents' rush to the hospital. I wonder which memory—mine or hers—was the one that stuck with my father as our family stood on the side of a hot Texas road bidding a sad goodbye to The Bug. The car was yet another casualty of our cross-country move to the Midwest, quickly sold for $50 after it broke down so that we could continue putting distance between ourselves and whatever had happened in California.

> We spent hours talking about how great the future would be. He said that he loved me. No one had ever told me that they loved me before. I was totally caught up in this world of his and worshipped his blessed aura.
>
> We talked about running away together, but then he'd remind me that I was a minor and that it would be a federal kidnapping offense.
>
> I believed he was the only cool person in the world. He turned me on to Tolkien, rock climbing, and folk music, and gave me my only window out of the cloistered Adventist scene that other teachers and pastors didn't. The value of that stands on its own, but the price I paid for that was more than it could possibly have been worth.

There are pages and pages more, details upon details upon details drowning me. More emails continue to pop up when I am least prepared; packages of typed letters even arrive on the doorstep, both of us seeming to find comfort in the reality of print. Among other stories, they include an account of her recently confronting my father about what happened. There are also reminiscences between herself and a longtime friend who was also in Dad's Pathfinder group. It is all much worse than I have been told, much worse than I could have ever imagined. Of course I was prepared for the difficulty of more physical details, but my heart sinks more with the evidence of my father's attitude: his intent, his awareness and conscious transgression. This man, my beloved dad, had been very much aware of good and bad and had repeatedly chosen wrong.

I want to say it is not true—I will it not to be true—but denial is impossible. Much of the information is laid out by her in specific, incisive correspondence from when she confronted my father and the administrators and conference leaders of the church he was lately heading. I comb the emails looking for his honest rebuttal, for his correction of the information, for the church's condemnation—but there are none.

I would even have settled for any indication of shock or outrage on the part of the church, or finding a sincere apology and acceptance of full responsibility from Dad, but there is nothing of that kind either. Just a final, backhanded compliment from him to Dr. Z: "I always knew you'd turn out great."

Nothing but practiced dismissals and vague promises from church administrators, and skirting and skating from my hero and seemingly everyone else's—the revered Seventh-day Adventist Church paragon, orator, preacher, teacher, pastor.

My father.

32

When she discovered my father had retired from medicine and returned to the pastorate, Dr. Z contacted the leadership at his church to state that he was a threat to children, that he should not be in such a position. After a lot of negotiations with Dr. Z—the Church always rabidly on guard against lawsuits and public exposure—SDA administrators grudgingly agreed to remove my father from that role and to ban him from preaching or, indeed, from holding any leadership role at any other SDA church ever again. In exchange, Dr. Z had agreed not to take her story public or to ask for reparations.

But not even a year after his removal, Dad had preached at another church in another town. His sermons were televised and posted online. A new church—not to mention that church's conference, which would have been aware of his appointment—was enabling, protecting, and promoting him yet again, blatantly disregarding his history of abuse and ignoring the women involved in their trademark dismissal. Dr. Z and so many other survivors had been sold to the wolves for the umpteenth time.

I felt horribly guilty by association. I sank with each batch of new information that arrived, each new email conversation. And there was a separate and dangerous undertow developing, too, a pull I couldn't quite define—a hint of competition, a "let me tell you who he is" tone where I felt Dr. Z correcting or dismissing my lifelong impression of my father, as if I did not know the real man.

And, of course, she was right—I had to face the fact that I indeed did not know him in some ways. I certainly didn't know the side of him that she had seen. But it deeply wounded me. We each held our own version of my dad to be the real version. Was the wonderful one I had grown up with a total pretender, a fake? It was crushing, devastating to question. Deep in my bones, I wondered if perhaps Dr. Z was right. Was my experience, my reality, my entire life an illusion? Was it all falsehood, smoke and mirrors?

I didn't know much about child predators, but I did remember a study that found predators often pick targets the same age as they were when they experienced grooming and assault or were similarly traumatized. I thought back to what little I knew of Dad's childhood. Pushed relentlessly through school by his parents, he was tiny and perpetually three years younger than everyone else in his classes. Short, shy, and precociously intelligent, he had been sent away to live with strangers to attend an Adventist high school at age eleven. The next year he went to an Adventist boarding school, locked away in a boys' dorm at the age of twelve, friendless, far away from family. I imagined the fourteen-to-eighteen-year-olds he had faced as a tiny preteen in the cafeteria, in gym class, in the locker room, in the shared bathrooms and bunk rooms on dark nights.

What happened to you back then, Dad?

I thought of every sex scandal I'd ever known about at Adventist schools—certainly no better than *those Catholics*. In fact, I tried to think of an Adventist school that *hadn't* had an abuse scandal that was whispered behind closed doors but never addressed, always shoved under the carpet.

The undercurrent from Dr. Z, fair as it probably was, then turned the lens on me: had I, too, been molested? She gently questioned whether I was hiding something, either subconsciously or purposefully. She was not alone in this suggestion. Every one of the few people I shared the story with suspected as well. I swore up and down, over and over to anyone who would listen that I was never, not ever molested in childhood by anyone.

But I began to doubt myself. How would I know for sure? People supposedly recover memories all the time. I found myself constantly defending my childhood, defending my father, sometimes to Dr. Z or to my husband and friends but mostly just in my head, feeling more and more confused and out of control. Never a good sleeper and still parenting two non-sleeping children, I began to suffer terrible insomnia and a whole new level of anxiety, ramping up a nightly drinking habit to deaden the fear of going to bed and waking up to some sort of horrible hidden incestuous memories.

I had opened this dialogue with Dr. Z. I had asked the questions, but I wasn't feeling any better with the answers; every new reveal made everything worse. It all made me nauseous, and I felt responsible—responsible both because my father had done awful things and even more so because I was opening up the old wounds. Even though I didn't believe in God anymore, I couldn't shake the guilt of ruining Heaven again for everyone—wasn't I?

I thought I owed Dr. Z. I felt she needed to see retribution, persecution, accountability, validation, acknowledgment, and not only had others failed to give these to her, I didn't know how to. I also didn't know what I needed from her. Whatever it was, though, I hadn't gotten it either.

I stopped communicating with Dr. Z.

I buried myself deeper in my sad cement house, my sad cemented life where Todd was no happier than I. We fought more and more. Ill-equipped to address our issues head-on, we never resolved anything. Eventually we fell into a cycle: building tension, eruption, then a patch-up and a return to separate lives and heavy drinking.

When our youngest was still a preschooler, we made a stab at family unity by buying a vacation house in Big Bear to make Todd's winter weekend trips more comfortable for all six of us. However, the house instead became the place where I escaped for the summers alone with a babysitter and my two children. I often stayed for a month or two, entertaining zero marital communication the whole while. I didn't even think to call Todd, and he apparently never thought to come up, even though he could make the round trip in a day for really good snow in winter.

I finally told Todd I wanted to reside at the mountain house year-round with our small children. To stay married, but just live apart. He was flabbergasted at the suggestion and insisted that one of us would start having an affair right away if that happened. It was my turn to be flabbergasted. The idea of an affair was utterly absurd to me and frankly sounded incredibly exhausting, a thing so far from my mind that I couldn't fathom it was something he could consider.

But I soon learned it was apparently on his mind a great deal.

33

"Who does Miss Lonely Hearts belong to?" hoots the cover band singer. Her question bounces off the empty dance floor and wraps around me with a whine like the noise a wet finger makes on a glass. My own glass sits before me, reproachfully empty, as I anchor a table next to the stage alone.

I give the singer a weak smile, expelling a little puff that I hope passes for laughter. I, Miss Lonely Hearts, belong to the man across the room at the craps table, the one laughing and carrying on with the woman in tall boots swallowing fat knees. I have no idea who the woman is, but they seem clearly more than just friends, she and my husband.

I stare at them. I stare at the band singer. I cast around for someone to meet my eye. The room is overflowing with people I know—I used to work for this company, too, before Todd and I had that mostly public "indiscretion" and left our spouses, got hitched, and had children. For tonight's festivities the company has hired a fancy mobile gaming company to set up a temporary casino in the top floor ballroom of a venerable old LA hotel. My former coworkers are putting on their best faux Vegas, rolling the dice as if their lives depend on it, attention so riveted on their pretend games of chance that they can't spare a look in my direction.

The atmosphere is festive and noisy, vibrating with the weird, nervy gaiety of most office Christmas parties: voices and attitudes just a bit too bright and engaged, action just a touch stilted. I had been so excited to be carousing again with this crew, the background players of so many of my happier times with Todd;

I had envisioned a return to our life-of-the-party early years—a date night reacquaintance with our effervescent pre-marriage, fun-loving couple-selves. Thus it was heart-sinking and entirely mystifying when the initial small talk proved to be so very small . . . so formal and awkward, shriveled. Almost immediately I found myself seated at an empty table in a string of empty tables, everyone else having quickly slunk off while my husband disappeared.

And now I guess I know why.

The band in front of me mechanically runs through their Sin City-themed repertoire, completely unnoticed and unappreciated by anyone but me. I can't leave my lonely post now, even if I had somewhere to go; I don't want them to feel neglected. They seem immune to the emotion, but I am not. I will smile, I will clap, I will be *cheerful*, even as my heart is being trampled over on craps table number five.

I like the idea of gambling but have never done it. I never even saw a real pack of cards until college. As Adventists, we could only play Rook, but even that was a little off-color, a bit risqué. Obviously a place called Sin City was not a place I had ever visited, and for the millionth time, I mourn the fact that I was forbidden popular music and TV and movies and secular novels growing up. Without a mental cache of proxy human experiences gained through pop culture saturation, I have no catalog of stored scenes illustrating my options for dealing with such an excruciating evening.

Fresh off of "Queen of Hearts," the band launches into "The Gambler." Even I, with two decades of gaping God-given holes in my popular music knowledge, have heard this song. I watch my husband and his friend link arms, giggle together, pick up their drinks and literally skip from one table to the next. They confer in whispers over the dice, her boobs spilling over his arm. Their new game begins with uproarious joviality.

I experience a stabbing memory of taking my blended family to visit my favorite uncle in Napa. My uncle worked all day, and I stayed at his home all day, caring for Todd's preteens and our two babies, overseeing naps and bedtimes, boredom and pool time, while Todd and my aunt spent their time gossiping, cooking, drinking, and grocery shopping together.

Had I seen *The Facts of Life* or *Happy Days* or *Three's Company*, or *Kramer vs. Kramer* or *On Golden Pond* or *9 to 5*, I might have had a cheat sheet for what could happen, for instance, if I confronted bad behavior. What if I strode over now and accosted the conspirators directly? Or what if I drank myself into oblivion and *then* strode over in a flaming hot mess? Or what if I grabbed the waiter and made out with him . . . or perhaps if I jumped onstage and belted out a blistering anthem of condemnation and revenge? Or . . . maybe I could storm out and end up on a *Thelma and Louise* road trip wearing multilayered scarves and lots of turquoise, burning sage as I sail through New Mexico in an old convertible?

I don't know how any of those scenes might actually play out because I was deprived of all dramatizations of real people problems in my formative years (Old Testament slash-and-burn piety and female sacrifice and submission don't count). Just as I cannot sing along to the cover band tunes or bond with their underlying emotions, I have no mental flash cards for potential ways to cope with my particular humiliation.

Or any humiliation, really. Or any average human experience in general.

So, alone with my thoughts and my downed drink, ice cubes slowly melting and heart fast congealing, I retreat into my only known method of conflict resolution: cheerful repression! I concentrate on the soothing ritual of counting months and years, calculating and recalculating, as I always do, the time until my children will both be eighteen and I can get a divorce. (I don't know why everyone always assumes that age is the pain-free marriage exit finish line. I suspect it's just as painful for everyone involved no matter when it happens.) On this night, as I massage the same numbers, I stare anew down the years-long tunnel of cement house family life and lonely parenthood wondering if the dreary march of time shall now include little Miss Boots gleefully ticky-tackying around the edges of my marriage.

The singer winks at me mid-song. I raise my melty glass. Another cheerful smile.

The buffet of Sin City recreations continues to rattle on around me, like that weird cup the dealers use to toss the dice. Drinking, dancing, rock music, gambling: the sounds of high stakes, high emotion, high life. People are cheering, people are groaning. I sip my melted ice and wish I knew how to play some of the games so I could join in, throw my cares on the table for a five-minute scrabble of win-or-lose abandon like everyone else. I've had nearly twenty years of life outside the church to accumulate these experiences, after all. I could have become a card shark, I suppose, but playing catch-up as an adult is tiring and time-consuming. Things other people absorbed casually throughout a normal life I have to seek out and study, like an academic. Do I really need to learn to play cards? Do I need to know how to operate a bong? Do I need to know the names of Charlie's Angels or the characters on Sesame Street or the members of the Rolling Stones? No. Mastering drinking and sex and old movies was good enough for me.

I think of the tiny children I left at home with the babysitter so that their father and I could have this rare night out together. I think about how I am tough with my children, unemotional. Todd criticized his first wife for being too soft, too indulgent, too accommodating to his first children, so goddamn it, I have aimed to please in that, like everything else. I aim to be the best at whatever this is I'm supposed to be, whether it makes a shred of sense or not. I am a specialist at this pleasing and perfection stuff, and I have learned to compete viciously with any other woman approaching my realm so I can get the man, keep the man, please the man, obey the man. I will *not* coddle my children. I will be better; I will not disgust him by being apparently weak and indulgent to my babies.

And I sorely, desperately miss those moments I missed, the tenderness I have denied both them and myself so that we could all be good, pleasing, obedient—so we would all meet expectations.

I get up from the table. "Where ya goin', Miss Lonely Hearts?" trills the singer. There is compassion underneath that sharp edge, I can hear it. But can't she see I am not up for the ribbing right now? No, of course not. I give a double puff of pseudo-laughter this time and a little wave goodbye. I'm very good at this faking thing.

I walk over to the craps table and inform my husband I am ready to go home. He turns to me, and there is an awkward moment filled with his pure shock and disorientation. It appears he has forgotten I am here.

As Todd and I struggle into our coats, Boots suddenly worms her way between us, rubbing up against him, flicking a look at me over her shoulder. "Goodnight," she murmurs with a shit-eating grin.

Boots clatters off. We head home.

The two of us are silent in his loud vintage car as we twist along the narrow canyon road nicknamed "blood alley" for its regular lethal accidents. When we both first moved to the LA area, there were no center dividers, no barriers on this route. Just head-on collisions.

I figure we might as well have one right now. I ask him if he is having an affair with Boots.

He doesn't answer, not really. The barriers are definitely up now. After a pause he tosses a poor substitute for one back to me. It bounces like a flat stone over water, dancing over the surface tension as if it has no weight at all until it suddenly, definitively drops out of sight.

"Wow," he says. "It's awful that you think that."

We swerve and sway around the sickening highway curves.

Just like a gambler, you gotta know when to walk away and

know when to run. The stone sinks without a ripple, and I suddenly know that I will run.

For that, I need some fancy boots of my own. I know just where to get them.

34

Those boots—a rotating wardrobe of tall and wildly colorful ones—were as exotic and outrageous as the swashbuckling, Gumby-legged cowboy who inhabited them. If Dolly Parton and the infamous California serial killer The Night Stalker had produced a Native American love child, it would have been Jesse Lavigne: notorious bull rider, actor, and Hollywood stuntman. Possessed of an impossibly outsized personality and dramatic lawlessness, his singularly flashy mix of wisecracking charm and chaotic energy almost—but not quite—obscured an alluring, black-eyed danger.

I had met Jesse the previous summer on a friend's vanity documentary film project: an old-fashioned horseback journey down a large swath of California where a dozen or more riders tested how much of the Old West trail system was still navigable by horse. Jesse was the project's wrangler and security boss. The sole rider to make the entire trip, he quickly became the star, just as he made himself the center of attention everywhere he went—captivating everyone with wild stories and even wilder behavior.

All tipping hat, "yes ma'ams," and flaring fringe, Jesse dripped with raw sex appeal. He vibrated with the most intoxicating, outrageous sensuality and freedom I had ever witnessed, and he had an endless number of hangers-on clamoring for his attention. Many of his fans stalked our journey by car and on social media, some of them even dragging husbands along. All of us on the crew laughed and rolled our eyes, but I couldn't honestly rule myself out as one of that number. I had fallen under his spell the moment we met the previous summer at the project's kick-off reception.

The riders had arrived on horseback to the historic ranch house hosting us, cinematically tying their mounts to a centuries-old hitching post near the verandah. Locking eyes with me before he'd even finished, Jesse strode past the fawning onlookers, head and shoulders above the crowd at nearly seven feet in boots and hat. Scooping up both my children in one arm, he took me by the hand and half led, half dragged me through the packed space to the stage where our team was being introduced to the crowd.

It was incredibly possessive. It was extremely inappropriate.

It was utterly electric.

We had spoken barely a dozen words. As I teetered giddily in backless Versace heels on ancient cobblestones, waiting for this strange adventure to begin, with this strange man holding my hand and my children, some long-buried thing deep inside of me began a silent scream.

The project spanned two summers, and I crushed innocently on Jesse from afar during that whole first summer, for which I served as administrative support from home. But after the disastrous Christmas party with Boots, and now well into working on my friend's project so many months later, I could not stop thinking of Jesse plowing through the crowd with me firmly in tow, my children in his arms, the sea of humans milling admiringly around him as he strode through like a raunchy, racy Moses.

Then and there, I decided to accompany the group for every inch of the film's concluding leg: a slow, two-month horseback crawl from central California to the border of Mexico. Later my husband would say I didn't ask. My friend would say I didn't volunteer. I did not give anyone a choice. I just announced I was going.

I took my first and second graders out of school, packed them into my station wagon, and ran away with the circus.

It was a bizarre, creeping caravan that for those few short weeks was the closest thing to safety and bliss I had ever felt since my fleeting nine months on campus at Barnard. After more than two decades serving as a minor supporting character in everyone's story, including my own, I felt the long-lost whisps of main character energy. People here valued my contributions, were interested in who I was, where I was from, and what I thought. I was seen, heard, and allowed to take up equal space and priority. Our tight production crew formed a mobile cocoon entirely outside the boundaries of normal society, nearly feral and deliriously happy—our food gritty, our skin grimy, our phones dead. The little band of riders, cameramen, and logistics crew lived on old-fashioned slow time, breaking rules and making waves like wild—but mostly benign—outlaws.

I dragged along huge binders of "makeup schoolwork" for my children that we never once touched until it was so cold one night at a campsite north of San Diego that we burned it all. We pitched it gleefully into the fire around which we had all huddled roasting hot dogs and s'mores, one of my few successful attempts at a crew meal.

Cooking had initially been my raison d'etre for joining the second summer trip: I could serve as cast-and-crew chef and unofficial mom, with the agreement that sometimes I could join them on the trail to log twenty-five to thirty miles of grueling ultra-run mileage. I had been so eager to get out on the road, however, that I overlooked one key fact: I didn't actually know how to cook.

At all.

My mother had clearly been a mediocre chef, and with eating disorders piled on top of restrictive religious dietary rules—no meat, no salt, no pepper, no spices, rarely any sugar—I had developed an early general disdain for food and whatever mysteries were involved in preparing or enjoying it. I had further had the great fortune of partnering with men who were magnificent cooks, which only perpetuated my kitchen ineptitude.

Unsurprisingly, my first dinner for the crew was a resounding disaster. On the flagstones of a historic barn and museum that was hosting us for the night, I labored over a congealing pot of gluey, overcooked pasta—with no second option. However, one of the has-been actors we attracted (they hoped our Hollywood producer would restore their dimmed star power to big-time, small screen success) had inveigled himself an invitation for the night with a present of wild boar. It was a gift for which I was so desperately grateful that I ignored his hand constantly brushing my backside as he seared the meat beside me on my tiny two-burner Coleman stove.

I served the exhausted, confused crew small bits of the savory pig meat next to my gummy, unidentifiable mess and retired in humiliation, berating myself in a corner of the old barn near a row of ancient buggies.

Jesse saunters up as I fight tears, puts his arm comfortingly around me. He tells me it's all okay, everyone's eating and my children are happily exploring the animal pens with one of the riders. I am so relieved and amazed that he knows exactly what to say before I even blubber about it. In an obvious but gratefully received attempt to distract me from my failure, he leads me over to the dusty old vehicles, and we poke around each carriage, each wagon as he regales me with glamorous stories of his adventures on similar ones over his long stunt career playing the stereotypical "Bad Injun." We climb into the rickety old cabs, imagining the long-gone dusty journeys—I picture prim, corseted, bonneted travel while Jesse envisions capture, revenge, and a wild dance of abduction and seduction. We crawl under a rusted suspension, admiring the horsehair stuffing of the seats, remarking on bygone passengers' small, uncomfortable accommodations, getting closer and closer—our hands "accidentally" touching. It is even more heart-stopping than it was in fourth grade when I watched a church-approved movie (*The Cross and the Switchblade*) with my "boyfriend" in the dark high school gym, dry-mouthed and shaking, hands dangling awkwardly between our chairs until they found each other in clammy ecstasy.

Jesse and I reluctantly finish inspecting the last vehicle and edge outside to the back rubblestone wall of the barn. Faraway voices echo from unfortunate diners still trying to choke down my meal as I luxuriate in the incredible knowledge that this glamorous, exotic man seems to like me—when I am suddenly lifted off my feet and crushed against the wall, cold stones hewn by long-dead hands grinding into my back.

My hair squeaks against the granite as he begins to kiss me, inhale me, consume me, electrically attuned and responsive to my every move, a vicious give-and-take. This man definitely knows how to clean a spoon. Violent and commanding, with all the ferocity and roughness I have always craved, his brutality instantly prods my sleeping dragon into roaring, fire-breathing ferocity.

Jesse spreads me out tightly against the stones, long limbs easily controlling mine, my flesh feeling each cold crevice at my back. His sharp-edged, rodeo prize belt buckle digs into my hip, and a giant, calloused right hand finds my throat. The grip makes my eyelids drop, like those tiny marionette-strung toys on push-button platforms; a little more pressure, and they will collapse convulsively. My breathing gets shallower as his tongue crowds out what feels like the last of my narrowing breathing space. I feel the blood pound against my eardrums, looking for an escape from the pressure in my skull.

I don't really know this man at all. Is he going to kill me?

The vowels in each thought stretch soundlessly through the sludge in my head, each *o* and *e* reaching out for the next syllable in a vain effort to stay organized. I will lose consciousness soon.

The dignified buggies behind him swirl in my dimming vision like a Victorian junkyard Fantasia segment, and I picture my body from above, espaliered on the stone wall. His hands tighten even further on my neck, each fingertip finding a spot to separate tissue from ligament: thumbs in parallel embrace over my voice box, index fingers along my pulse. Can he feel the blood fighting to get through?

Does he like it? Do *I* like it?

I need it.

Adrenaline surges through my system, replacing fear of the unknown with that familiar, delicious terror and surrender. I heave back against him, bucking, writhing, biting. He clamps down harder. Dizziness makes the far-behind space spin in cotton candy fuzziness. My limbs feel heavy and weak, disconnected from my body.

I haven't felt this in a couple decades.

I haven't felt this ever.

Not like this.

I am seeing spots now, and I don't know if my eyes are open or closed—there are little exploding points of light while all I can feel is his mouth, his tongue, his breath, his huge, rough hands. I imagine my throat stretching out like the women with stacked neck rings that used to mesmerize me in *National Geographic* magazine. Like them, I will suffocate when released because I'll be unable to hold my head up.

But I already know in the marrow of my numbing bones: there will be no release for me.

My children are out there in the extended barnyard campsite with everyone else. I am married. This is very, very dangerous territory.

But there is no returning from this point. I have found someone who will own me completely.

35

From that moment on Jesse and I were consumed with each other. He was like nothing and no one I had ever known.

We spent every possible waking moment together, bonding, dumping out our life stories. As the trip wound down from a few weeks to mere days left, we grabbed every possible second to be alone: talking, sobbing, clinging desperately to one another, trying out every configuration of any potential future in which we could continue to see each other. He swore that I was his only hope in escaping from a bad relationship, a horrible life; I had arrived just in time to redeem him from a dark and sordid past, a dull and loveless future. He said I was his saving angel.

He had given me a new lease on life as well. Not only did he live life on the edge, one hundred percent present all the time, but he treated me like no one ever had. I had felt intellectually connected to my first husband and socially connected to my second, but never both to one person. With Jesse, it was magically, impossibly *all*. He seemed to like everything I liked, and we talked and laughed and laughed and talked. He was solicitous, protective, and incredibly attentive—swearing to live and die protecting me, staring into my eyes for hours, hanging on my every word, noticing even the smallest things about me and complimenting them. He seemed to genuinely give a place of honor to me and my interests, enthusiastically ready to participate in my life goals and passions instead of assuming my allegiance to his.

And I *knew* it must be true love because he had fallen for the raw, bare-faced me. I had rarely worn makeup on our trip, and he had found me valuable anyway. If that wasn't proof of true love, what was? Even my own mother had not been capable of it.

I felt valued and cherished like never before by anyone, ever, parent or lover. It inspired me to hope I could still be and do whatever I wanted because no matter what it was, it was clearly not going to be half as outrageous as Jesse was. There was no judgement with Jesse: no bad, no wrong. Being around someone who was so absolutely okay in the face of disapproval—with breaking a rule, with being different—who thoroughly bucked conventions, deliberately thumbed his nose at society's frown . . . if he could do it, maybe I could too? I finally believed in soulmates. Nothing seemed to matter but figuring out how to be together forever.

Our crew had all joked that we just wanted to keep running when we reached the border, cross into Mexico to live the lives of outlaws and never look back. No one wanted this as desperately as Jesse and I. The closer it got, the more I dreamed of it: finally crossing an arbitrarily defined boundary, having permission to let go, to go. I willed it to happen on my last long run—another unofficial ultra-run of nearly thirty solo miles through the beach towns north of San Diego while the group on horses trailed far behind me.

We would all break up and go home in two days. Aside from those few early years of college freedom, this six-week film production had been the only time when my life was directed by me, according to my interests, my desires. And now it seemed I could possibly have both: a man who adored me and my own interests, desires, and life direction? I could not imagine anything even resembling a life without Jesse.

I began to sob and stumble, experiencing for the first time outside of an airplane a full-fledged panic attack—choking, hyperventilating, dizziness. As the edges of my vision closed in and I dropped to my knees in the city, my last thought was random but reassuring: *I know the Marines take training runs around here.*

Maybe one of them will revive me.

When I came to my senses—legs numb, torso hooked awkwardly over the beach-path railing—I knew I had not been revived by man, medic, or Marine, but purely by my own misery. As the feeling slowly returned to my ribcage and the air to my lungs, I knew: I simply could not continue in my colorless life, living for everyone else's convenience, any longer.

———————

I am getting divorced. Again.

The woman across from me looks bone-tired. Disappointed. Angry, even, though mostly resigned.

It is a look shared by all the other lawyers in the courthouse volunteer advice office—I don't know what it's officially called, but that's what it is. If you need to sort through your divorce but you can't afford or simply don't have an attorney, you can ask them for help doing the paperwork. Today there are only women working here, both lawyers and paralegals who volunteer their time to help people like me protect our rights and not get screwed.

But we are all resolutely getting screwed here, in spite of their long volunteer hours and best efforts. I can tell this lawyer is infinitely sick of, sickened by, people like me—women like me—coming for help and then not taking it. Refusing to protect our rights and defiantly screwing ourselves.

I left my marriage almost immediately after returning from San Diego, blithely reassuring my shattered and deeply wounded children—and myself—that it was really better for me to be a happy, loving and loved half-time mom than the bitter and lonely full-time mom and housewife I had become. I made no attempt to reconcile or work on the marriage. My ex immediately found a new relationship, too, but he is bitterly angry at me and very vocal about the fact that he thinks I should walk away with nothing from the marriage due to my betrayal.

I want so desperately to make nice, to be good and helpful and to atone for my sins even as I am committing them, that I have gone along with everything he says. It is his right to have these emotions, after all, isn't it? But this kind, patient, overworked woman is trying to show me that it is also my right—my obligation—to protect and provide for myself and my children. I can see I frustrate her endlessly.

"Who is the primary caregiver now? Who drives them everywhere, who picks them up?"

"Me . . ."

She puts her hand on the papers. "You know that doesn't stop when you get divorced."

"But we're splitting custody, fifty-fifty," I counter. Sheesh . . . has she even read those papers under her hand?

"Do you get paid for all of that now? For all that time and all those extras?"

"Well, no . . . because we have an agreement that I stay home and take care of the kids and Todd works. Plus, nobody gets paid for being a mom . . ." Is she being purposefully obtuse?

"Okay, but you need to be paid for it going forward, see?" I can tell she is trying to stay even, measured. "Because none of that is going to change—you will just be the primary caregiver without the primary earner financing it. Those are the roles you took on: he is the primary earner, and you are the primary caregiver. If you let him off the hook on his end, you're still on the hook on yours. Forever. Divorce doesn't change that. That's why we have these recommended formulas."

Pfffffft. This woman. She wants me to be one of *those* women. The ones who expect motherhood to trump everything else, who can't suck it up and support themselves.

She shakes her head. "You don't want to do this. I can tell you, you don't want to do this."

She is trying to will me into sensibility; I can feel the energy in her body radiating it at me. She shows me my meagre income from self-employment as a writer and eBay reseller—cobbled together, it makes just a tiny bit more than minimum wage. Then she shows me my list of expenses. She shows me my soon-to-be-ex-husband's six-figure salary, his multiple houses, his stock options, his retirement accounts. She tells me there is a simple formula to calculate it all. It's not personal, she argues, it's mathematics. He owns and makes this, you own and make that, so this is how much you need to receive.

She reminds me that I have not had a job outside the house for over a decade since I have been raising all four of the children. I set my full-time work aside and helped with Todd's side business instead; I dumped savings into toys and real estate that supported his passions; I committed time, money, and resources to our future at his family's homestead. She reminds me that I am driving hours every day for our children because I cannot afford housing close to him and their school, which prevents any normal job schedule.

I tell her not to bother running the numbers.

Todd has made himself clear that he doesn't think he should pay a dime. I all too willingly agree. I fell in love with someone outside of my marriage, and so I am a harlot, a bad wife. Deserving of stoning, public humiliation . . . or at the very least undeserving of support in raising our babies. There may or may not have been boots in his closet, but I am clearly at fault now, and I have to pay for it.

I warn her that I won't even look at the numbers. I'm not going to use them!

I know it will say that I should get a lot. I know that from when Todd went through the same numbers and negotiations with his ex-wife long ago. Ten years later, I am settling for even less than what he paid her, and I am also refusing all spousal support, even though I'll qualify for it for life by the time our divorce is finalized.

I took Todd's side against his first wife then, and I take it now against myself.

I've been bred for this, groomed for this, and I know just what to do. Men shouldn't have to pay child support or spousal support! Weak women! Dumb women! I will turn against women, myself or any other, in favor of men. I will take the man's side, instinctively, vehemently, even when they won't appreciate it and it will really hurt my children most of all.

The real shame is that neither of us in this divorce war is thinking of our children. Todd seems to be angry and hurt and to want to punish me while I am trying to do penance and desperately avoid all confrontation, all unpleasantness. But the woman across from me *is* thinking of the children, and she is not pleased.

She knows what happens. She knows that I am (and will be for the next decade plus of split custody) forced to live in the cheap areas far outside the city center, which will drain me of tens of thousands of productive hours and dollars in gas and lost work opportunities as the only parent to drive the children back and forth. I am the parent who will make the round trips to retrieve the nighttime comfort stuffie, the book report left on the kitchen table, the forgotten gym shirts and cell phones and school projects for children struggling to manage themselves between two houses. She knows my children will grow up in jaw-grinding material insecurity and financial fear, afraid to ask for basic things—school clothes, birthday parties, a trip to the movies—because Mom's face will crumple when she says she can't afford it.

My volunteer lawyer looks into the future and watches my children offer up their piggy banks when they ask for a bagel. She can see them struggling to make and retain friends because Mom's house is too far away, and they are left out of spontaneous parties and playdates. She watches them turn down activities and invitations and sports tryouts because Mom would have to drive more. She can see them staring into the sack lunches on their laps as we sit in my car, trying hard to ignore friends streaming by on their way out to eat because they know I don't have the money to send them with the group.

She feels it as they swallow their needs, marinating in constant anxiety, because she knows from experience that children have no capacity to understand that Dad's generous salary and real estate portfolio balance out Mom's poverty where it concerns them and that they will be okay. She just hears the fear in their little voices when they ask, "Are we going to be homeless, Mom?"

Her voice wavers. "Basic financial equality exists for the children. Security and safety *for them*. Equal opportunities and circumstances in both houses, *for the kids. That* is why you take adequate support. It has nothing to do with you."

I am making a lawyer cry. She can feel their pain, and it makes her mad. She is so angry at me—at all the stupid women like me who walk in and out of her door every day, shortchanging our children's comfort, our own psychological wellbeing, and our chance to become independent by denying that we deserve financial support after decades of free labor, denying our own access to it just so we won't cause a problem. So we can be nice and pleasing and cooperative.

She hates us for being the biggest enablers and instruments of our own destruction.

But I refuse to listen.

She refuses to sign the papers. She says I need to think about it. She says I need to come back later.

I don't, and I do. I eventually creep back in and find a random person with fewer opinions to sign the papers for me.

I am divorced a few days shy of our tenth anniversary with no spousal support and woefully inadequate child support that will a few years later be set to zero.

36

Legal matters were about the last thing on my priority list, however, as I was high as a kite on my new life. I moved into my own place, a beautiful old house in the middle of California's many agricultural fields. Several months later Jesse roared up, hell-bent for leather, in a pickup truck after some sort of police-involving breakup with one of his long-term girlfriends. He'd told our film crew he had two girlfriends and a wife but swore to me he had jettisoned them all immediately upon falling in love with me—except for the wife, he later allowed, who had been that in name only through several subsequent decades and uncounted subsequent relationships so that she could keep her legal-immigrant status. I didn't question any of it; he seemed as all-consumed with me as I was with him; it would surely be impossible for either of us to have any bandwidth for others from here on out.

I decorated the house in a beautiful display of the convergence of our cultures: Jesse's beaded traditional dance regalia on the carved mantel above my grandmother's trunk, the faux tomahawks from movie shoots next to the painted nesting dolls my parents brought back from mission trips to Russia and Belarus. I hung drawings of Jesse by famous artists above my antiques and settled his tooled Western saddles under my fancy Latinate college diploma.

We had done it. We belonged only to each other now.

I was barely able to eat or work, so taken was I with Jesse's sudden overwhelming presence. He was everything I had been raised to shun and came with everything I had always wanted: a fascinating Hollywood career, glamorous friends and travel opportunities, and constant, terrifyingly rough sex. I was head-over-heels for him, and he was outrageously, possessively in love with me too, wooing me endlessly with tens of thousands of poetic texts and notes—hundreds per day—promises to take care of me and my children, invitations to movie premieres, film contract riders stipulating that I be flown out to join him on set. He was publicly, physically affectionate and demonstrative, and I felt he was proud of and with me.

His magnetism drew people in everywhere we went, pure idolization from friends and strangers alike, and it was heady and intense. People he had just met gave him their family heirlooms. Artists begged to draw and sculpt him, street-style photographers chased him down for photos. Oscar winners gave up their afternoons to attend screenings of his indie films or bring their families on set in weather over one hundred degrees to watch him do crazy danger tricks over and over again to get the perfect shot. He was a stunt world legend, still taking ratchet jerks and horse falls and car hits. Worshipful crew members would sidle up next to me to whisper, "We all fight to get into his set van . . . Jesse is amazing."

I, too, was finally a main character in my own story. I started to blossom physically and professionally, scoring magazine writing gigs in local glossies, my opinion pieces quoted in books and blogs. I met Hollywood contacts and began working on a feature screenplay that eventually won awards and notice. I got fitter and stronger than I'd ever been, running ultramarathon distances with ease.

Through it all there was more sex and danger than I had ever dreamed: complete abnegation that utterly effaced me, debased me. Jesse was Satan, sin, and sex all rolled into one package, and I could not get enough. It was not roleplay; there were no discussions or permissions. There was only scarily painful, not-sure-I'll-live-through-this sexual violence that at various times injured my hamstring, broke my nose, caused internal bleeding, and gave me constant bruises and tender spots along with the strung-out exhaustion of our constant, voracious activity. We were both rather proud of the evidence of our passion. When we needed even more adventure and variety, we paraded our way into Nevada's legal brothels for adventures in multiples. Mutually insatiable, we goaded each other onward: sex on airplanes, in parking garages, in other people's kitchens, in an old truck pulling a horse trailer eighty miles an hour down the highway with a giant bus of foreign tourists gaping alongside us.

For several ultra-vivid, heart-stopping months, my wildest dreams seemed to have come true in a whirlwind. We galloped around the world together, from film sets to premieres, Las Vegas blowouts to bull-riding championships, US Embassy parties to courtside seats. I could not believe that, in my *forties*, I was actually walking the red carpets I'd long ago ogled in *People* magazine at the Michigan Public Library. I was giggling on set with Christian Bale about a horse farting throughout a long take; I was posing with an Italian superstar at an embassy party in Berlin. I sashayed through film festivals, hung out in base camps and makeup trailers, and accumulated blue check friends. The promise of a wild and interesting life that I had only glimpsed at Barnard had arrived with a splash, and I was entranced.

But, of course, it wasn't all perfect. I knew true love required hard work, and I was a really hard worker, so I worked to ignore the small insensitivities that began to crop up—so hurtful and jarring in their contrast to the over-the-top love and glamour. I had little OCD tendencies—arranging the eggs in a carton symmetrically, never using the microwave on uneven numbers—that Jesse invariably made a point of flouting. Despite declaring he loved my writing, he never read anything I wrote, even when I gave it directly to him. He tossed it onto the coffee table and left it untouched until I eventually threw it away. He would lust graphically after a

TV personality until it visibly upset me, and then would casually turn on her show whenever I walked into the room.

Sometimes disappearing for days or weeks at a time, he would return with no explanation, muttering and shouting in his sleep hints of dark adventures and secret work. On motorcycle rides, he would terrify me, splitting lanes and swerving, leaving me in tears and hyperventilating. I learned to sit woodenly and give no indication of fear; I refrained from tapping him or squeezing tightly because he would immediately speed up and get more erratic.

If I spoke up about any of it, he was invariably shocked, even a little disgusted—how could I be so childish and sensitive over how many eggs were in the carton? How self-centered was I to insist he read my work? How could I expect him to know what he said in his sleep? Why was I even *with* him if I just wanted to go the speed limit, color within the lines?

It always made me feel so silly when he pointed it all out. Of course, he was right. I was being petty and childish and unreasonable. It was so stupid and small-minded of me to sweat the small stuff because I was unbelievably lucky that he had chosen me. We were soulmates, after all; we loved all the same things. What did I have to complain about?

Life was really, overall, so incredibly grand and beautiful.

On the surface.

The only place I knew how to live.

Lurid, oversized vaginas and vulvas and penises—vivisected and rendered in unnerving 3D gray-and-denture-pink coloring—taunt me from the walls of my gynecologist's office. Why are the illustrations of our most human elements always so unnatural? Take the

Kama Sutra: is there anything so ridiculous? As an eighteen-year-old new sexual initiate, I undertook a massive hunt throughout rural Michigan to find a copy. My prize, finally unearthed from the bowels of a Chicago thrift store, insulted and sourly disappointed me, the greedy scholar, the overachiever: I had quite obviously fallen for a cheap, bloated marketing scheme on a multicentury scale. Not only were the illustrations thoroughly idiotic, but their claim to elucidate sixty-four different ways to have sex was patently perfidious. There were only slight, often minute changes to the angles, directions, and limb positions indicated, even to just the attitude of the toe, from one silly drawing to the next.

As I wait and squirm and burn, staring at genitals magnified, I ponder the overall ridiculous simplicity of sex, yet more aggravating proof that there is no God. When it comes down to it—hah, pun upon pun—sex is a pretty limited, repetitive set of practices using the same small areas and fragile parts. We are the only members of any species who try to pretend it is outrageously diverse. Cowgirl? Doggy? Missionary? Whatever. If an intelligent being really created this whole mess, she would have gifted us with significantly more varied responses and outcomes and wildly versatile body parts, perhaps a little tougher and more multiuse, for truly wide-ranging and prolonged sexual enjoyment. I picture each human as a different weird Swiss army knife of fleshly apparati that could possibly simultaneously squirt, suck, grow, vibrate, engulf, whatever. But alas, no. All of us sad, cookie-cutter, bipedal creatures are endowed with the same two implements that loom over me in excruciating detail here at the doctor's office, our few basic portals and appendages upholstered in thin, fragile skin that tears, abrades, and dries out so easily.

None of that is what brought me here, however.

There are many pains and injuries that come with rough sex, with lots of sex, and with lots of rough sex. I have felt them all. The furious desire, that rabid drive to transcend myself and obliterate my history—if just for a few frenzied moments—could, and often did, break my body in various ways. It resulted in muscle failure and injurious collapse; severe dehydration of delicate tissues; friction that removed layers of skin; cramping, bleeding, or numbing; and dizziness or occasional blackouts. There are, it turns out, far more ways to accumulate bruising, abrasions, punctures, and scrapes during fornication than there are sexual positions, that's for sure.

But this burning sensation, that did not come from rough sex. It came from dishonest sex.

Huddled in my fiery hotseat, I am overwhelmed with deep shame and abject horror. Shame that this could happen to me, horror that he *did* this to me, knowingly—the man who claimed I was his angel, who stared into my eyes for hours, who said I had saved him from certain death, who swore he loved me beyond his own life.

Afraid of this very problem, I grilled him about STIs when we initially hooked up, and after full sexual contact with Jesse, I had never slept with my husband again for the same reason. Jesse had sworn he was clean, and I would never have been rude enough to push further; I would never question something like that said to my face. But I had still put off actual sex for the longest time, like all those Christian virgins-by-technical-foul, proud of their purity even though they had made up more ways to sully themselves than the Kama Sutra ever could.

Only hours ago I came to Jesse after a sweaty-palmed google search, kneeling beside him in his habitual prone position on the couch watching TV. "Jesse. I need you to be absolutely honest and truthful with me."

Even in the desperation of that moment, the request bounced hollowly between us: a ridiculous pipe dream, more ephemeral than if I had shouted it into the ever-present bong beside my man. But I plunged onward, pretending, as we always did, that he would absorb and respond to information like a normal human being.

"I need to know from you. Right now. Is there any reason why—*any reason in the world*—why I would suddenly have a . . ."

I choke on the words, and it suddenly becomes very important to use the correct ones, the precise terminology, as the acronym has changed since I was a teenager. My official sex education consisted of being told masturbation caused disease, listlessness, and stupidity; that little pieces of me would be given away to every man I slept with until I had nothing left; and that women didn't ever want sex but had to put out on demand at all times for their husbands or it would be their fault if the men strayed. So, I had eked out a bare-minimum knowledge from the teen magazines in the library, a blessed few of which had actually covered STDs, which were not called STIs until decades later.

That seems important at the moment. Important to one of us, at least. "Is there any reason why . . . I would have an STI?" I whisper.

We both know it cannot have come from our brothel visits. They all scrupulously maintain multiple layers of protection, from genital inspection of all patrons to weekly testing of workers and strictly observed rules of contact and condom usage.

Jesse blinks at the TV, blinks at me. His face arranges itself in cascading, lightning flashes: slightly annoyed, slightly offended, slightly incredulous. It settles into an exaggerated, blank confusion, as if I am speaking in tongues and he cannot begin to decipher what I'm saying or why I am asking him, of all people—as if I had suddenly expected him to know the velocity of a meteor.

"Huh." He scowls sullenly and steadily at the screen again. I wait, and he grows increasingly annoyed that some other answer is expected. "Huh. *No*." His gaze does not waver from the television. "No, not that *I* know of."

I get up and leave. I go to the doctor. I come back from the doctor. I stalk numbly around the house, throwing things in bags.

I do not tell him what I think I know. He should know what I think I know.

But he pretends he doesn't.

Instead, he follows me around the house, looming over me, swamping me with an always spinning, slightly threatening kaleidoscope of emotions, throwing out prickling shards of indignation, menace, desperation, and indifference like police tack strips under my feet. "What? What does this mean? Wow. Does this mean I need to go get tested? Huh? I guess I better go get tested!"

It is so accusatory and so heavy on that *I*, the verbal italics of victimhood. I continue to pack grimly, silently. The protestations continue as he tests the gamut of emotions for which outburst might arrest me: surprise, fear, anger, blame. He makes forceful, rapid-fire postulations: he is clean; his ex-girlfriend has set him up; I must be cheating. He loudly, histrionically professes complete ignorance and unfamiliarity with this weird and foreign problem. He pretends he has never heard of such a thing, did not know anything like this existed. He threatens furious retribution against "whoever did this."

He offers to swear his innocence on his mother's grave, but quickly retracts it out of selfless consideration for her. It would be unfair to dredge up her poor dead soul to disprove such an obviously untrue, vicious smear on his character. He owes it to her to rest peacefully as she knows him to be absolutely blameless, but he *would*, he *could* swear on her grave if he needed to.

I leave. Again.

I go to a motel for a sleepless night.

37

Jesse calls several times with all the forced sniffles and tremulous voice of the implied cry, the dry cry. He is so scared, he says. He has never heard of any of this, he says. He doesn't know what is going on, he says. This is such an unexpected, unfair crisis, assaulting us both out of nowhere, and we need to stick together now more than ever; we need to unite in fighting and denying this mysterious enemy.

I hang up. I lie in the cheap, motel-issue synthetic sheets and watch, unmoved, as the invisible cellophane descends over my head, my mouth, my eyes and nose, my battered body. "Do you want to be the shirt, neatly in the package?"

I feel the pins sticking in me now, invisible trusses to create that perfect front. This time the pins are not in my arms and neck; they are in those private parts that have been poked, pinned, possessed, and preyed upon in all women before me, everywhere, forever—little unforgiving pricks of domination over those poor private portals belonging to half the world's population, through no fault of our own, that the other half seizes, uses, and commands through *every* fault of their own.

After a sleepless night, I drive home to face my obvious fate. Jesse appears contrite and eager. Maybe because he loves me, maybe because he missed a single night of sex, maybe because he is afraid his meal ticket is over. I ask him why he didn't fly in terror to the doctor yesterday, as I did, if this is all so new and scary and mysterious to him.

He is cornered, shock arresting his face in a micro-minute of desperate calculation that I have only seen from him a few times. He flattens, he flares, a glitch of expression, a schism between what might be true and what is pretend, leaving him with no ground to stand on.

But he recovers. He expostulates that he *did* go to the doctor. I watch in dumb awe as his bravado builds, his sentences compound. He *did* go get tested; he was forced to get tested because of *my* problem. He splutters with indignation. It was terrifying for him. *His* results were negative. It's a *me* problem.

But he has no vehicle of his own, his truck having given up the ghost months earlier, and I have been gone overnight, only for a few hours at that, and so I haven't even gotten my own official results back—they take seventy-two hours.

I know he didn't, and I know I'm not the problem. But of course, in the end, he simply, obviously does not care, so it *is* a me problem. Here I am: simply by trusting that my relationship was monogamous and my partner truthful, every bit of my childhood programming returns to crush me. I haven't believed in the idiocy of purity culture for decades, but I have become, at long last, that wrinkled, soiled shirt on the floor. I am the chewed gum, the licked cupcake, the masticated chocolate bar, the denuded rose, the crumpled bill. I might as well stay in this relationship because I have become those damaged goods after all. I shudder at the hopelessness of it all.

When it's hammered into you that your only worth is your sexuality, the details don't really matter. Prim virginity or defiant sluthood, whatever; two sides of the same coin. It's all still the only currency that defines me.

A week later my results come back: negative. Even the doctor seems surprised.

I do not believe them—the doctor had warned me that inaccurate results are quite common—but I test again and it comes back negative again. Years later I will learn that I am allergic to silicone, a ubiquitous ingredient in sex toys and lubricants. It is the latest in a long string of mysterious allergies and outbreaks that I have exhibited repeatedly in times of stress, beginning way back with Matt Sanders's assault. But I won't put that together until much later. At the time, I simply believe I have made myself a despicable castaway, just like they preached. I am dirty, I am undesirable, unclean, used.

Jesse jumps immediately on the attack, furious with me for putting him through such an unjust accusation. He does not care what might be wrong with me, how or if he might have contributed, or when he might pass something else on to me. It is my fault; I have done him wrong. It goes on and on, and I feel smaller and smaller until I sense I've become entirely invisible. There's no longer enough left of me to exist inside of. Instead, I watch myself from the outside as I crumble. Yet again, layers of dishonesty, chaotic emotions, half-truths, turned tables, and accusations have transformed something I think is true into a spectacle of my own irrational selfishness. This time, my deeply personal issue has been made suspect, laughable, and irrelevant by Jesse's outrage and hurt feelings.

Does it really matter what the truth is or whose fault it was? I am utterly confused, but one thing is clear: by accusing Jesse of hiding other relationships from me, I have made things worse, much worse.

I apologize. Profusely. Abjectly.

But the damage is done.

Just like that, Jesse owns me more completely and thoroughly than church and marriage ever have.

From then on it was clear that the power dynamic had been cemented. I would accept and endure any abuse from Jesse, and we both knew it. He did not hesitate to use it, escalating my confusion and uncertainty and regularly wringing tears from and instilling fears in my little family. Wrangling and catering to his needs became my new raison d'etre, and my service was unending, my nervous system locked at a four-alarm status.

Our relationship continued as a constant storm of frenetic activity and high-adrenaline glamour suffused with alternating bouts of effusive love and wicked cruelty. The months grew into years, and I learned to focus on the highs—doing anything, spending anything, allowing anything, ignoring everything—to keep upping the ante because terrifying lows rolled in fast and furious.

All of the times, both good and bad, from mundane household expenses to extravagant big purchases and even those secret trips I couldn't ask about, were always on my dime. Jesse's disappearances were now often blamed on some offense committed by me or my children that drove him out of the house, but they became increasingly trackable via social media—celebrating a faux wedding anniversary with his ex, cozying up in Los Angeles or Toronto or Santa Fe with random women. When he tired of the latest rendezvous, I would receive a phone call with indignant reasons why things weren't as they appeared. I was just being unreasonably jealous: the photos were old, the women were stalking him, the compromising positions were just for show with costars. Then he would demand a return ticket home.

Under the guise of being an open book and having nothing to hide, he put me in charge of all of his accounts. It was such an honor—he was trusting me with the intimate details of his life! And then suddenly he was incompetent, couldn't remember anything, didn't know how anything worked. If I insisted that he do things himself, I then became the whipping post if anything went wrong, which it inevitably did because he couldn't be bothered to answer, save, or remember anything. It was so much less traumatic if I just did everything for him myself, so I became solely responsible for answering his email, remembering all his passwords, setting up all new accounts, managing his banking, arranging his auditions, and submitting his self-tapes. I ran his social media, I drove him everywhere, made his travel arrangements, ordered his supplies, picked up his medicines and custom horse gear and mail.

Whenever I tried to break it off and kick him out, he created a debilitating emergency—the loss of his phone and wallet, a health crisis, the theft of his truck, a blown-out knee, bankruptcy, an ex-girlfriend that had put a hit out on him. And just when the chaos and cruelty threatened to overwhelm me completely, Jesse would suddenly show great vulnerability and giant gestures of affection. Days or even weeks of the solicitous, attentive man with the enormous, delightful personality and flamboyantly demonstrative love for me would follow: hundreds of love notes and doodles once again tucked into egg cartons, under my makeup bag, in my running shoes, accompanied by sporadic, over-the-top social media posts expressing his undying devotion and adoration.

My will to parse the bewildering mix of love and lies, connection and manipulation, had been broken at this point, and I grew to dread the euphoric times as much as the abuse, because it only made waiting for the other shoe to drop more painful.

And often that shoe dropped in the middle of the night.

38

I feel the heaviness before I hear the hiss.

"You better get ouuuttt. Nowwwww."

A heavy, deadweight flesh blanket drapes over me, immobilizing me, that familiar yard-long arm and bony leg surprisingly weighty. I remember this feeling comforting in the beginning, the way we slept when he started talking in his sleep. There was once such a magical safety in burrowing beneath him as he murmured extravagantly foreign, unintelligible things, his lips at my ear.

"You better leave if you wanna live!"

I stay very still. I wonder if he is awake or asleep. I can never be certain.

But I know not to move either way. If I can maintain total stillness, feign a coma, I can sometimes evade what's coming. I am transported back to my teenaged years playing possum while my father stalked me for the hated wort-chip time. I inwardly shudder.

"AAACCCAAAAAAHHHHH!" It's a guttural scream, directly into my ear canal, and I flinch in spite of myself. His spit settles in a fine sprinkle across my cheek. The shock of a war cry mere inches from your ear drum is nothing next to the creeping, ugly feeling of saliva sliding slowly into your eyelashes.

At first Jesse's unusual nighttime monologues had been unbelievably seductive. Wrapped naked around me, long limbs dwarfing and cocooning me, he had talked in his sleep almost every night, a fascinating and exotic mix of Sioux, Comanche, and English, punctuated with incoherent mumbles. The dramatic, unintelligible expostulations were always tantalizingly laced with alluring professions of undying love for me, whispered half-hints of dark crimes committed in the name of honor, adorably nervous practice marriage proposals ostensibly addressed to me, and one-sided conversations with unseen beings—all scrambled with moans and mutterings, salient words only partly decipherable, intermittently distinguishable.

I was so incredibly, deeply honored to have this open, unprotected window into his soul. So many women wanted to be, fought to be where I was, but only I had this uncensored look into the tough guy disarmed. Only I was so lucky to be trusted with his sleeping, unguarded thoughts. I would lie awake every night, breathless, waiting, listening . . . hoping I could piece it all together and make sense of him and his confusing rollercoaster emotions, desperate to hear anything that would reassure me that he really did love me.

"*Fuck* you! FUCK YOU!" His knee drives up into my thigh, causing an immediate cramp. I fear the gig is up, but I still try to keep still.

Jesse's once enchanted mutterings have slowly morphed over time, like all his other behaviors, from charming and seductive, winsome and protective, to petty, unpredictable, aggressive, and terrifying. He has reached a new low with these cloaked physical assaults, this psychological torture that he has made into an art form. The dangled half-proposals have more and more mixed with cackled warnings and threats, and now the garbled night oratory is used only to hurt, to test what hurts: pseudo-confessions about other women, exclamations of defiant unfaithfulness, insults directed towards my kids, my spending habits, my drinking, my friends, my race, my aging, and my mode of dress.

Confronting him in the morning does nothing—of course he is not responsible for what he says in a dead sleep! How *dumb* of me! It is diabolically perfect, like every other torment he has devised: he can say anything and deny it later. He does not remember, it isn't important, it isn't true. Am I really so insecure and stupid that I take any of that seriously?

And . . . gosh. I guess it does feel stupid. He must be right. Right?

He sits up. I tense.

Things have progressed to the point that every time he's awake, I have to be awake. His defiantly unmanaged diabetes disrupts his sleep, and he is awake a great portion of every night. Howling over some petty injury, demanding back scratches and help sitting up, wandering around his studio banging into things, slamming doors and lids and cupboards, flipping on lights, turning on the television. And talking, always talking: "I'm outta here, I'm done! This just ain't fun anymore! Fuck it!" He can afford this midnight chaos; with no set work hours, Jesse's days and nights are interchangeable, and he takes many long afternoon naps. I, however, must be up in three hours to face my customary fourteen-hour day.

That hardly matters when he has a burning question for me now. "Did you tell that guy when to come?"

I am momentarily stumped, and then—oh. Crap. Today they are filming a documentary on Native Americans and horses featuring Jesse. I think I forgot to tell the director it would be good to come at feeding time, around 7 a.m.

Jesse begins angrily flipping through the Robert Grahams in his closet—expensive, colorful print shirts with contrasting wild cuffs that we have made Jesse's calling card using my credit card.

"This is bullshit. I'm not wearing this, there are no pockets!" He throws shirt after shirt on the bed, a thousand dollars of brightly colored cotton. "Get rid of those. He doesn't even make sleeves long enough."

These are all gifts from me, purchased with money I cannot afford. Some I found at thrift stores, but some were bought for hundreds of dollars on trips I financed to Las Vegas, Carmel, or Los Angeles. And it hurts. Even though I have come to expect these insults, it hurts. He has begun to turn on my presents, finding something suddenly wrong with them months or even years after happily accepting them, discarding them now with disgust and outrage.

He stomps into the bathroom. I start crying.

Our day has begun.

By that point I had tried many times to break up with Jesse, but I always let him return. I gave in to his temporarily reformed behavior and protestations of undying love and dependence, his emergencies and crises that only I could fix.

I told myself nobody understood him, nobody understood our relationship. It was true, nobody did, not even me. I convinced myself I deserved the mistreatment, that I had brought it on myself; I had fallen in love with a man who apparently wasn't what he pretended to be. It must have been all my fault. I had cheated and abandoned my modest life for wild sex and a wild life. My wayward Eve body and soul had condemned me and my children to this fresh hell.

Not only did I tell myself that I deserved it, I fantasized that I loved it. That I loved how everyone was mystified by our relationship. I loved being a rebel, I loved living beyond the borders of conventional life.

Sometimes I did love it. Sometimes I was scared to death.

Sometimes I loved being scared to death.

And sometimes that was the worst feeling in the world.

After several breakups, patch-ups, and moves, we had all ended up living on the farm where Jesse was general manager and wrangler. It was the only place I could afford, and I was lucky to have it, but it was the last place I wanted to be by then.

My children and I had three rooms in a dilapidated structure on the property, which we shared with a bunch of twentysomethings, while Jesse had his own studio. I didn't like being in a college dorm setup or under one roof with Jesse, but I literally had no other choice: rentals in our tiny town had always been expensive, but prices had skyrocketed after a series of wildfires destroyed a huge portion of the housing stock. So I tried to see the best in our situation.

The property was a fairly typical coastal California oddity: a multimillion-dollar trash heap with a lowbrow Grey Gardens vibe, owned by a deeply eccentric mother/daughter duo I immediately, of course, dubbed the Edies. I adored the handful of low-key fellow renters, and the kids and I were close to town while getting to enjoy being on a working farm. I started a garden; I learned to milk goats and feed horses, to chop wood, to drive a tractor and pull a trailer.

For a refreshing change, when Jesse first got the farm job, his ire wasn't vented at me. As soon as he had moved in, he started fighting with the farm owner, Big Edie. He stormed about and left nasty voicemails and texts whenever she was a few days late with his weekly salary. She took to tiptoeing around doorways and corners of her own property after those explosions and asking me in whispers to check Jesse's mood before they would begin a day's work. Any time she had to talk to him, she would funnel the message through me. She was generously providing both a home and a job for him, and he seemed to revel in biting the hand that fed him: he would repeatedly burn up the engine of an old truck because a brand-new one was off-limits; he would cut down old vines Big Edie revered; he even secretly sent off for a DNA test on her horse to prove that it was not the rare breed she thought.

I struggled constantly in the middle for peace, once again the unwilling filter between Jesse's cruel outbursts and the rest of the world, and he delighted in watching me scramble to fix or minimize them. He threatened to stuff newspaper in the old house's faulty wiring every time we left town, and over the ensuing months I suspected he had a hand in the death and/or injury of several animals, but I couldn't definitively prove anything. He was always one step ahead of me; everything turned out to be either made up or covered up, and I couldn't ever be certain which was which.

Then the onset of the pandemic in 2020 created a dramatic, immediate distance between us and the Edies. I cheered its arrival, believing it would bring welcome relief from my role as intercessor. However, now deprived of multiple targets and general drama—stuck at home like the rest of us, with no chance to make secret mercenary trips, run off, cheat, or go on drug benders—Jesse turned his focus back on me and my children. Again.

I had no padding of denial or delusion left. I knew it was not love, had never been love on Jesse's part. I dreaded the abuse, the lies, the thankless demands and angry commands, the rages and violent threats. I was sleep-deprived, full of fear, never fully able to predict what would be inflicted upon me next.

I stopped showering, I stopped getting dressed; I wore the same clothes day and night, a week at a time. I gained twenty pounds. I tried to cope in cold sobriety for six months, then went back to drinking myself into shaky numbness at night. If I didn't absorb, deflect, or hide all of Jesse's actions, we could *all* get kicked out of our housing, and I had nowhere to move and no money to do it with. Jesse knew he had us all exactly where he wanted us: totally controlled, tiptoeing around him.

As the pandemic subsided, the Edies became omnipresent, which was seemingly the last straw for our beloved housemates. Freed of lockdown and only too happy to escape the tension, drama, and upheaval both inside and outside the house, they moved out. A few months later, Little Edie announced she was moving in. I was paralyzed in the knowledge that she would soon be exposed to Jesse's behaviors 24/7 and I would again be put in the middle or held accountable more than ever. I knew things were about to go horribly wrong.

And I was right.

But, for the slenderest moment of hope, I thought I had a chance. Jesse went on a movie shoot in Europe for a month and ended up hospitalized after some sort of bender. The time and space without his oppressive presence emboldened me. I could not hold my secrets anymore and appealed to the Edies. It was the first time I had ever told anyone what went on behind closed doors.

I shared only the broad strokes about my fears: the abuse, entrapment, his threats—I figured they had experienced enough of his abuse themselves that they would understand. I knew they had known about his hard drug usage, in addition to suffering his screaming rages, and they knew that he had kicked Little E's dogs—and those of her friend. He had threatened the dogs so viciously and repeatedly that Little E had at one point moved all the way out of town for a while.

Despite the relief of unburdening myself and the hope of help at hand, my own troubles were still scary and shameful to unload. It was excruciating to finally voice even a small portion of the horrible details to anyone, but I was desperate. My ability to hide any of Jesse's aggression and volatile behavior would end with Little Edie's move in anyway. It would come down on me in one way or another, so I might as well be honest.

I begged the Edies for help.

I asked them to kick him out.

Two weeks later I was served with an eviction notice.

39

"Get out get out get out get out!" The voice of my teenaged son mobilizing his online video game troops floats down the hallway. The knot in my stomach finds kinship in his urgency—someone on his crew obviously snafued.

Through the hazy concentric circles printed on my curtain sheers, I watch the Edies stalk back and forth through their garden in floppy hats and stained khakis, cackling at each other in their own made-up language. One of the dogs circles, yapping and snapping. The slight breeze ruffles the bullseye print in front of me, and the mother/daughter pair floats in and out of focus, a *Deliverance*-edition James Bond opening sequence.

"Dude, you better not hang around! Get *out!*" my son urges his digital soldiers.

Get out indeed. I have seen so many animals and people cycle on and off the farm as though through a revolving door: picked up, celebrated, supported, then sidelined and vilified and shed in situations of bad blood. For so long it all seemed slightly odd but personally harmless . . . until the regular ouster activity towards tenants, workers, and friends finally came my way. Now I am being blamed for everything I confessed about Jesse.

Somehow, I didn't see this coming. Somehow I never thought it would be me.

I shut the latest flaming email without answering. It is only the most recent in a series of rambling, accusatory addresses taunting me with my problems with Jesse, accusing me of making up my fears and fabricating the danger he is to me and my children, as if I'm creating some kind of sick game. I had never before told anyone about his behavior, never trusted anyone with the shame, the terror, the humiliation, and now to open up for help only to have it turned on me . . . I am stunned.

I contemplate fighting back for a moment. I could dig in and play dirty, go public with unsavory personal secrets and leverage the Edies into a renewed lease, I suppose. But, sadly, I can also understand how Big Edie doesn't believe me—I always put on such a good face. And I don't have the stomach or energy for another war. I am barely hanging on as it is, and as usual, Jesse's behavior has become bigger, more dramatic, and more all-consuming than ever. Plus, I have a growing, insistent feeling—a tiny but steady voice among all the other oozing, off-gassing, strangling, festering whispers forever drowning me under my surface. It insists that this might all be a good thing. If Jesse had been doing such cruel "little" things to Big Edie, a friend who supported and employed him—how badly must he truly have been treating me?

Right now I just need to get out of my room, but the only door opens into the house's shared kitchen where the Edies will soon be carrying on their banter, masticating cheese and avocados and almonds, open-mouthed, as they chatter.

"Get out, man, get out! What are you waiting for, an invitation?"

My boy has found his own escape from this madness shut up in his room, capitalizing on a preternatural self-possession and nerves of steel—coated in years of his own childhood trauma—that have made him an ideal war game commander.

"Go go go, they're on you, man!"

I jump up, grab my laptop, and scramble furtively down the hall as the kitchen door opens behind me. The Edies burst into the house through one opening as I flee through another towards the lesser, or at least the more familiar, of the evils currently plaguing me. Jesse's latest strange hospitalization has not toned down his hostility or abuse, but I am used to his. Theirs is new and confusing, and my wounds from it are still raw.

"Don't look back, dude, just *go!*"

I dart through the door of Jesse's studio and drop into the duct-taped office chair at his wobbly table—both of them farm relics. He's in his customary position: TV blaring, bong in hand, watching ghost shows.

It is all suddenly too much. I start bawling. And then—

"This guy you want me to work with, this old friend with the TV show. Is this somebody you fucked?"

The air goes out of the room. I look up, choking on nothing at all but the oxygen that won't do what it's supposed to do and slide down my windpipe. That filmy, swimmy feeling—is it in my eyes or in my throat? "What? Who? What are you talking about?" I am seeing spots now, but in a second I realize what he is saying. "You mean my sister's friend who wants you to consult on a film?" Now it hits me: I have jumped into the wrong foxhole. I ran behind enemy lines. "Umm . . . I dated him briefly thirty years ago. Does it matter?"

Of course it does.

The roaring assault begins: the accusations of infidelity, the looming and stomping and hurling of insults, the slut-shaming, the transference of every wrong he has ever committed against me onto me. He doesn't care how long ago or how little loved the encounter, nor how potentially lucrative and career-forward the job for him might be. He won't serve a man who has touched me, and I'm a whore for suggesting it.

It goes on and on. But I don't hear it, not exactly. Instead, I silently review the endless times I've had to sit and make nice with his various conquests at end-of-show parties, in makeup trailers, on sets. How I've had to pose in the middle of brightly lit, awkward red carpet sandwiches: him, me, and his latest bedfellow, all of us hitting our best three-quarter angle—chins up, chests out, arms around each other—"Over here, over here!" Smile. Click.

I can't catch my breath, can't even lean on the table for support—like everything else around here, it is shifty, unstable, unreliable. I double over. My own knees are the only safe space.

There had been a different war going on—there *is* still a different war going on between me and the chortling people in the kitchen who are planning to evict me however they can—and like all skilled abusers, Jesse knows to attack on an unprotected flank while I am weak. Here in his studio, it has come down to sex, as it always does. He is dragging up this thirty-year-old fling and beating me with it because I recently told him I was unhappy with our sex life.

Not just unhappy; I have come to *hate* the sex. I have faked everything all through life, but the breaking point, when it happens, always comes down to sex. Eventually my resentment seeps out like sewage under a door, reeking and running over everything in its path, and it drags the whole structure of my life off its moorings.

The intense emotional connection I once believed Jesse and I had was long ago obliterated by his defiantly paraded infidelities and callous abuse, and my usual rampant desire has been slowly crushed by a repetitive, self-serving ritual of his. Sex with him has slowly deteriorated over ten years from the most mind-blowing, body-consuming, soul-shrieking, boundary-pushing, endless adventure to rote routine: the exact same moves in the exact same order every time, with me in service to his needs, my face buried under the tent of his legs, my body anonymously exploited.

For months now I have been gritting my teeth and rolling my eyes under yet another 69 position, literally choking myself silent to keep the peace, tears sliding down the sides of my face to pool in my ears—nearly my only unmolested orifices. It all invariably taunts me with Ben Franklin's "Advice to a Friend on Choosing a Mistress": pick a mistress with good legs, because those last the longest—even if she gets old, you can just put a bag over her head and do your business with her less aged parts. Anybody can be just any body if you sit on its head.

My head has been sat upon for too long.

I had the computer clutched on my lap, but it now slides to the floor with a soft thump. I have ceased to hear and now simply watch Jesse's rant. Everything is disjointed and unconnected—his words, my nonresponse—like peering through binoculars before you pinch them together to merge the input, with both eyes trying in vain to make sense of what's in front of them.

We know that our eyes actually take in all images upside down and our brains somehow turn them right side up. Why the extra work, I wonder; why don't we just learn to live in a world where everything is upside down?

I picture waking up tomorrow terrified like I did this morning, like I do every morning: bullied into wakefulness by Jesse's baleful nastiness, still madly trying to figure out how to placate him, how to resolve this latest blow up and stay with him, how to continue gamely on with this rote sex, smashing down my revulsion, my outrage. I picture the reality of us moving out to live elsewhere under one roof: a miniscule, thin-walled apartment crammed with Jesse, myself, and my two almost grown children, four people with distinct personalities and needs. I envision trying to pay for it all—the rent would surely be double what I'm now paying—while Jesse sits on the couch, filling the tiny rooms with stale pot smoke, loud demands, and constant reruns of ghost-hunting and Bigfoot shows. I see the kids and myself tiptoeing through the haze, sneaking out fearfully like we used to do when Jesse first moved in with us, afraid to wake the sleeping monster. And I watch us all eventually get kicked out because of Jesse's gleeful, deliberate flouting of rules: destructive alterations, threats made to neighbors, domestic disturbances.

I run in mental circles trying to figure out how to manage all of this in order to please a disruptive, unpredictable man who has no credit score, no driver's license, no job, no savings, no steady income, and no desire to change any of that—only to make it all more and more my responsibility.

"Get out *now*, dude. Don't wait, they're coming!"

The words come down the hall, around the corner, echoing everywhere, boomeranging off different chunks of my life that only now will answer back. Finally, all at once, with great force.

"Go on my command. We're gonna run for it."

Dear God-all-fucking-mighty who doesn't exist. *Do I have to?* I'm so fucking tired of running. So tired of running.

"Here we go! On my count! Ready?"

Yes, my son. Just one more time. I'm ready.

"One—two—three— RUN! GO GO GO!"

And I do. I rise up from between my own knees.

I am done.

40

Like all births, there was no going back.

I told Jesse he was not moving with me. I would not carry him, I would not support him; I would not be his service animal anymore. I would no longer absorb the lies, the betrayals, the bad moods, the breakdowns, the drama and chaos and abuse. I would no longer put him above everyone else. I would no longer protect everyone else from his behavior.

I didn't care what happened to me. I didn't care if I was homeless, I didn't care if I had to go live with my parents. I didn't care if he killed me.

I was done.

I rented the first thing I could find: a tiny apartment far out of town, an excruciating commute away from our community. I gave my children the two bedrooms, and I slept on a makeshift couch in the living room with the cat. Once again I spent my days locked in traffic most of the time, ferrying my kids to their lives thirty miles away, and despite my efforts, they were often stranded far from their friends.

But it was ours. Ours alone.

And I was on my own for the first time in my adult life.

My independence was easier said than done, of course; my departure from the farm was only the beginning of a long, excruciating, and unpredictable process of repeatedly prying Jesse's tentacles off of and out of me. He used and reused every trick in his book: he blew up, pretended there was no breakup, made himself in desperate need of assistance, blew up again, had another health crisis, threatened me, bribed and wooed, threatened to kill himself, suffered meltdowns, and then came more threats, more health crises, more blow ups, and beautiful love letters.

But I did not give in. I did not look back.

I had no time to lose and many decades to make up. Relationship-free for the first time ever, I threw myself into an artificially induced whole-life coma. Flying in the face of all common sense and good advice, I changed everything I could think of, all at once, throwing out the good and the bad equally. I vowed to completely deconstruct myself, this person who was still just trying to cope. I would take myself apart piece by piece and examine each building block to identify where it came from. Was it forced upon me? Was it built up as automatic, defensive armor? Was it a simple knee-jerk reaction of rebellion? Or was it a proactive and healthy personal choice?

This reevaluation was a conscious decision, intellectualized rather than felt, as had always been my habit: I would deprogram myself, approaching it clinically and systematically, peeling myself like an onion, starting with the most recent events and digging backwards toward my childhood. Soon enough, however, I had to face the fact that my body and my emotions both had to come along for the ride.

In order to see and feel everything clearly, I quit drinking. I dumped my calming kratom extract and CBD oil down the drain. I started therapy with a woman certified in religious trauma and high-control religions. I went on long walks and hugged trees. I inhaled piles of self-help books. I began journaling, dumping my life out in notebook after notebook. I started meditating. In my apartment I sat for hours and days in a terrible and unfamiliar aloneness, with no numbing devices to take away the pain—no thrill-ride relationship, no alcohol, no hippie stardust, no abusive sex, no bingeing and purging, no cutting, picking, pulling, chewing.

At first I could only see the bad, the horrible things I had done and patterns I had repeated: the people I had hurt, the terrible choices I had made (many times when I lacked a choice) again and again. The accompanying ugly emotions surfaced over and over, a waterfall—a flood, a swamp, a quicksand of shame, regret, anger, self-loathing—and deep, deep sorrow. I watched it all roll through me, uninvited, unregulated, feeling it all for the first time, constantly reminding myself to allow it to happen, to let the awful feelings exist. These previously forbidden, unruly sensations often completely overtook me: scary, foreign, and relentless, they ripped through unbidden at any given moment. I bawled when I said goodbye to my children at school. I sobbed into the racks of $4.99 skirts in Goodwill. I broke down over high school marching bands, cat videos, and the gnarled hands of old women squeezing avocados at Safeway. I raged at stupid tweets and people who drove too slowly. I screamed when I couldn't get the lid off the tomato sauce. I lay comatose in bed unable to move for hours.

It slowly dawned on me that all these buried, real feelings now uncontrollably surfacing were why I had always been called "fake" by classmates and why I was a thoroughly mediocre actor. Why I had for a long time refused to listen to music or watch serious movies. Why I never kept a journal before. Why I could never "make love." I could only put on a fairly convincing display, an ever ready demo of the happy emotions—the pleasing ones, the ones I knew were acceptable and nonthreatening. Those were the only ones I was allowed as a child.

Other feelings, the "dark" ones, the "selfish" and illicit ones—I could only skim over those. I could not let them in. When I was growing up, there had never been any safety for showing negative emotions, particularly strong ones. They drew shame and occasionally violent discipline. For most of my adult life I had filled the vacuous space they left with effervescence and enthusiasm, yessing and pleasing on a turbo scale during the day and numbing myself into a stupor every night with any self-abuse available because I wasn't safe expressing or even feeling my own needs and big emotions. I drugged, drank, fucked, cut, or starved them into silence so that the people who controlled my space—the men to whom I submitted completely in place of the authority figures of my youth—weren't inconvenienced or displeased.

What started in my formative years—choking down and internalizing all conflict, questions, shame, and desire in order to blankly obey, please, and fawn as the perfect "good girl"—led to an adulthood, I am even only now realizing, entirely without boundaries. I was as doggedly desperate to please and appease my children's friends as their teachers, the telemarketer on the phone, my hairdresser, or the man in my bed. I looked for external direction and approval in all things.

In particular I had been throwing myself directly under the feet of controlling men, internalizing their minutest moods and opinions as direct commands, shoving the reins in their hands so that I could perform my regular scramble—what was "comfortable" for me—of trying to anticipate and match what they needed, wanted, judged, felt, or thought. Having been raised with the steel-toed boot of familial and cultural dynamics pressing down on my neck, crampons buried deep in my flesh, I had not known what to do with my brief tastes of freedom. I had always reverted to the familiar pressure, always looked for more boots under which to trap myself. Even with a man who didn't consciously want that control, my second husband, I turned the good guy into a bad guy by putting myself in a no-holds-barred support role and devoting myself to living his life in his house and his town, socializing with his friends, encouraging his hobbies, raising his children, planning to live in his family home . . . and then raging at and resenting him for it.

Then eventually I found the ultimate alpha male: the zenith of demanding, debasing, requiring my endless self-sacrifice, someone who took without limit and with no remorse at all, cult leader of a one-on-one cult. I obediently allowed him to wreak destruction on everything important in my life—my money, my health, my sanity, my self-worth, and my family—until it broke me. I knew that the man I fell in love with was not even remotely identifiable as the man who ended up throwing shoes at my head in the middle of the night, but that did nothing to ease the guilt and recrimination of it all: how did I, a smart woman, fall for such nonsense? And why in the world did I stay and enable and support until I was entirely consumed, barely clawing my way out in time?

The truth revealed itself slowly and painfully, in stages. Through gentle hints from my therapist, strategic counseling posts forwarded by friends and family, recommended self-help books, and randomly discovered YouTubers, I discovered the lists of behavioral traits of psychopaths, of narcissists, of people with Cluster B personality disorders: Impulsive behavior, pathological lying, lack of remorse, failure to accept responsibility, early childhood behavioral problems—check, check, check, check. Stimulation seeking, grandiose self-worth, recklessness, parasitic orientation—check, check, check, check. Controlling others with threats or aggression, a tendency to physical violence, entitlement, arrogance, emotional instability, dramatic erraticism, using charm and charisma to manipulate—check, check, check, check, duck, duck, goose.

Every single box ticked off and the profiles aligned with startling precision—not a single trait missing on any clinical diagnostic list of red-flag behaviors for these diagnosable disorders. I began to remember the tossed-off comments Jesse made many years into our relationship once his grip on me was absolute: he had failed the Armed Forces psychological evaluation; he had a psychology-major ex-girlfriend who had written her PhD on his "personalities." I had dismissed those comments, like so many others, as just part of his personal myth-building. Everyone loves to claim they're crazy at some point, right? I had never studied psychology—Adventists don't believe in it, generally, as everything can just be cured by more prayer—nor had I ever entertained the idea that Jesse might really be mentally ill. Certainly his medical records—as thick as an entire set of *Encyclopedia Brittanica* from all his bull riding and stunt work—attested to the fact that he had sustained more concussions and brain injuries in one lifetime than an entire football team. But I had never known there might be an actual diagnosis or that other people knew and had named the exact behavioral patterns I had struggled so futilely to make sense of.

I finally had a clear but devastating picture of the danger I had been in and how narrowly I had escaped. The flood of relief in knowing there was an explanation for Jesse's behavior did nothing to ease the blame I heaped on myself for having been duped onto such a damaging path in the first place, however. The shame and regret I felt for spreading chaos and ruin in my little family, no matter how unwittingly, remained. I continued to question how and why I had been so susceptible to such outrageous abuse, and the difficult emotions returned over and over again: sadness, depression, hopelessness, embarrassment. But as I continued to look inward and backward, peeling that onion, I entered a new stage, encountered a new feeling. A dangerous feeling.

It was rage.

Rage, I learned, is different than anger. Anger pops up as a momentary response to something, a reaction to a specific provocation. The rage rolling over and through me felt like a timeless element, a bottomless reservoir of fury so engorged with repeated injustice that its burn would not go out.

I had spent my entire life directing that rage impotently, inwardly towards myself and my body or towards those I loved who were unable or unwilling to fight back. But the rage boiling up within me now could not be redirected. It knew exactly where it was going.

For thirty years I had lived a determinedly secular life, a rabidly not, Adventist life. After I left the church at eighteen, I had not entertained a single thought about it—I was not angry or anti-Adventist then, I had just flatly refused to acknowledge it in any way. Both religion and the weird and embarrassing past it had gifted me were dead to me, they had nothing to do with me.

Or so I had thought.

Now it was becoming obvious that I did not turn into a pawn for narcissistic abuse of my own accord. There was a reason I had sought it out, why I had fallen so fast and hard for manipulation, guilt, gaslighting, terrorizing. The abuse itself, even if it came in different forms or a different context, was comforting. It was home. It was how I had been raised. In Jesse I had not only found the abusive cult leader I had been bred to follow, but his street misogyny directly mirrored my ingrained biblical misogyny: women exist to serve and be used.

Now that I recognized this, the rage boiled over, self-righteous rage—the only righteousness I was ever going to pursue from here on out. I was going to see it all the way through to the end, no matter how ugly and messy and brutal it might be.

The SDA church and I had a score to settle. And for that, I needed to revisit an unexpected source.

I needed to go back to Dr. Z.

41

I hold it gingerly, that fat manila envelope I have carried from house to house to apartment, never reopening it but always acutely aware of exactly what and where it was—that loaded pile of email bombs that stripteased across my computer screen fifteen years ago, potent little grenades of awful revelations between Dr. Z and my father, Dr. Z and the church, Dr. Z and myself, Dr. Z and other church predators.

I have always known I would eventually have to open this envelope again. During the last six-odd months of grieving and screeching and flailing through my peel-back self-discovery exercises, I've been circling around this chunk of papers like a Mexican hat dancer around the hat on the floor. Eventually I had to stop tapping my feet and waving my arms and striking poses and actually pick the damned thing up.

I have to put it on my head—I have to put it *in* my head—and keep dancing.

When I first found Dr. Z, I thought she could give me all the answers. My dad had only told me a fraction of the truth, so her revelations had been life-imploding to the point I had assumed they would be the key to figuring out everything about my family, my upbringing, my issues. I'd always idolized my father, after all, like everyone else, so if I could just figure out how and why he went so wrong, then I could make my life make sense. Dad's dethroning and the church's duplicity must hold the answer.

But in my recent process of unrolling the tightly wrapped ball of my life, as I pull the inflamed and tangled strings into semi-sorted, messy piles, it becomes clear that Dr. Z's story—their story, my dad's and hers—is really not a big part of mine. I had thought she would somehow fill in all the holes for me, the ones I knew were there but couldn't even name. However, it turned out that trying to solve this one situation—one instance of church abuse, even if it was within my family circle—would not address the larger issues, the systemic issues, the structural issues, or my personal issues.

Ironically, though, in generously giving of her experience, her reflections, her growth and hindsight, Dr. Z indeed gave me the answers. I was just looking for the wrong ones.

I slowly open the manilla envelope. It is sun-bleached on one side from a long exposure sitting near a window in some room at one stage of my life or other. The pages inside are just as I remember: dozens and dozens and dozens of them, long, conversational passages, single-spaced. I flip through them quickly, sliding out page after page, over and over. There are no page numbers, and I don't know how I'll get them all back in order, but I can't stop—I want to see them all. I vaguely remember—I think?—that there is a lot of random information Dr. Z wrote about the church in these messages that I completely ignored.

She had been trying to give me the perspective I so desperately need now, but I hadn't been open to the bigger picture she was painting. I didn't want to think or talk about church at that time—nor do I now, to be honest—so I had blown it all off. I had put her messages under a microscope, circling certain parts, trying to squeeze meaning from my father's every move or word, just wanting to understand how my beloved dad could be such a bad guy, but I had purposely ignored the rest. I so blithely believed myself purged of Adventist influence and out of their reach that in the original shock of connecting with Dr. Z, I had focused solely on my dad, on her, on how *their* story might affect me. Anything else to do with the church literally made me nauseous; I had been gagging and flipping off SDA churches as I drove past since I was eighteen, so I did not give a rat's ass for the context, the history, the background that Dr. Z laid out in detail. In struggling to absorb the entirety of the situation I had barely even taken note of the pathetic official wrist-slap for Dad and the shoddy cover-up I originally attributed to them; I had not remotely absorbed the awful complicity, endorsement, and outright enabling of the Seventh-day Adventist Church in the whole mess. I certainly hadn't connected all that to anything currently happening to me.

Now I want the whole truth.

I skim, I scan, I settle in. Things start to pop out at me. Rereading her notes hits much differently today.

Combing through our correspondence with fresh eyes, I am reminded that once Dad's abuse of young Dr. Z was initially exposed, a series of other unscrupulous Adventist pastors, teachers, and counselors shamelessly piled emotional and spiritual abuse on her. The fourteen-year-old was discredited and told it had all been her fault. She was instructed in no uncertain terms not to ruin the church's reputation or my father's standing—and all while being sexually abused *again*, by several other men in the church.

It was unbelievable. It was indeed systemic.

Likewise, my mother had been commanded by her own mother and by the Adventist church elders to accommodate her husband's peccadilloes in silence. She obeyed, suffering through a miscarriage that was surely at least in part stress-related—although that was never acknowledged—as she joined the astonishing number of people in the community who knew and didn't do anything to protect the young girls in Dad's orbit. All told, there were dozens of enablers: a pastor who yelled at Dr. Z to leave my father alone; a church leader who suggested she undergo female circumcision; the entire seminary board who voted to ordain my father after his multiple scandals; and the church conference that continued to desert, betray, and gaslight Dr. Z while allowing my father to join their preaching roster.

Now, as I review these accounts, instead of feeling frozen and buried under someone else's trauma, thinking I personally need to fix the situation—to understand, apologize for, and make up for my bad dad—I see that Dr. Z never put that pressure on me. I thought she did, but I put it on myself. She had already held my father to account quite eloquently on her own behalf.

She was not guilting me. She was not asking me to make it all better. I felt the rage in her, and it scared and awed me, but I didn't know what it was then, and I didn't know how to deal with it. On the crumpled, tearstained pages I can now see clearly that she directed her anger at what has affected both me and her—even Dad—the most: the Seventh-day Adventist Church.

She never aimed that rage at me. She was handing it to me. And now I'm ready to take it.

After all, the dad I grew up with is not the one Dr. Z knew, but the church we all grew up in is definitely the same. And it has screwed us all.

42

Dr. Z and I both quietly entered the Instagram deconstruction community during Covid, when we were all desperate for social connection, and had silently begun following each other. After I read through our correspondence again, I reached out to her. We began talking once more. I read and reread those original emails, and I asked new questions.

I gritted my teeth and read, sometimes through tears, often through waves of nausea and rage, the materials Dr. Z pointed me toward long ago that I had been too overwhelmed and too self-absorbed to review the first time around. Now well-versed in the ins and outs of narcissistic abuse, I marveled at how the God of the Bible was portrayed by its writers and, by extension, the Church and White. They all used the exact techniques and exhibited the same behaviors as classic narcissists: alternately love-bombing and mistreating those in their control, manipulating everyone to consolidate their own power. I choked and fumed over Shryock and his hateful purity manual, *On Becoming a Woman*, which I had loathed in high school but never read completely. I highlighted and screamed at its recommendation of female circumcision to cure masturbation, its completely fabricated explanations (from a medical doctor!) for homosexuality and the terrible effects of premarital sex. Through chats on Instagram messenger Dr. Z filled me in on Dr. Shryock's gross backstory: he spanked his own sixteen-year-old daughter for wearing lip gloss, and he performed and endorsed sterilizations without consent, some of which were inflicted upon Dr. Z's own family members by Adventist doctors.

I tracked down a BBC documentary in which an ex-Adventist woman talked of her circumcision at the age of three at the hands of an Adventist doctor—and when she returned to an Adventist physician in her teens for the resulting discomfort, she was summarily dismissed, her only "treatment" being a manual on resisting masturbation. Dr. Z and I jointly wondered how many "undesirable" girls underwent sterilizations and circumcisions at the behest of Shryock, who for decades was the dean of medicine, writing all the training manuals, at the celebrated Adventist medical school, Loma Linda—the same institution attended by all my family members and Dr. Z. How many SDA women were out there blaming themselves for never becoming aroused, never orgasming, never getting pregnant—confusedly performing for years their unending, God-given duty to please their husbands, feeling it must be their fault that the experience left them barren, cold, and unmoved?

Through Dr. Z I also learned that Adventists were the first and loudest to champion conversion therapy. They financially backed and gave generous podium time to pastor and conversion therapy advocate Colin Cook and his various offshoot organizations, continuing to promote him and other like programs in spite of repeated abuse scandals, legal prohibitions, and countless studies proving the practice was harmful and did not work. I thought again of Jill, my locker neighbor, who disappeared as a swaggering, athletic girl with sparkling eyes and a ready laugh only to creep back months later as a mute, skinny, joyless Holly Hobby. I learned that the Adventist Church was complicit, through their leaders in several religious-political advisory positions, in aiding and abetting a law in Uganda that made homosexuality punishable by death. I watched as the SDA Conference president instituted a "human sexuality task force" that would not take questions or church member input but existed solely to reassert the primacy of "traditional, biblical" gender roles and marriages.

I began looking at all the research that had been published regarding Ellen White since I left the church: books and websites and ex-SDA theology students on reddit reporting the most shocking realities about the revered prophet. She plagiarized much of her writings from others, and her "visions" were often copped from another spiritualist at the time or targeted to attack a congregation member she was warring with. Even her much-revered health message was authored by others—Drs. Kellogg and Sylvester Graham and, before them, Samuel Tissot. She did not even follow her own injunctions, regularly eating shellfish and meat and, reportedly, having quite a relationship with alcohol (and, according to some, opium).

White regularly punished church members by publicly outing their sins. She also advised a member caught abusing a young girl not to tell anyone about it—not the police, not the church leaders, not even his own wife. One particularly interesting rabbit hole led me to investigate the traumatic brain injury she sustained as a preteen when clubbed in the head with a rock by a classmate. I learned that her particular area of damage, the frontal lobe, often affects the part of the brain that controls joy, making sufferers of such injuries unable to experience happiness or pleasant emotions. Furthermore, such brain trauma can result in Geschwind Syndrome, which manifests in seizures, hypographia, circumstantiality, hyper-religiosity, rigid thought patterns, and atypical (usually reduced) sexuality. Even a casual observer of the prophet's lore would immediately identify all of the above as distinctly Egg White behaviors.

To help process it all and vent some of that rage, I began posting in the deconstruction community, the word "deconstruction" referring to dismantling the human constructs of religion—a concept I had not previously known existed. There were a few ex-Adventists in the space already, but as with every other place I had ever been in, identifying as anything related to SDA was a pretty lonely endeavor. I initially started talking about what a weird church I grew up in: the multitude of strict rules, the claustrophobic environment. But it was impossible to talk about the church without also getting into its many off-shoot cults—the Branch Davidians (and then David Koresh as part of that group), Marcus Wesson, the Ant Hill kids—or criminal members like serial killer Robert Lee Yates, not to mention masturbation-phobic Kellogg and Shryock.

Nearly all of those stories led back to the church's many sexual obsessions, so I began talking about the scandals I remembered: one at my own academy after I left; the tragic case of molestations and suicides at Monterey Bay Academy that had kicked off my acquaintance with Dr. Z; a friend's dad who had an "affair" with his student; a relative relieved of his teaching job due to an "inappropriate" relationship with a young girl. In googling to see if any of the cases I remembered were public, I simply entered "Seventh-day Adventist abuse" and was left utterly speechless at the returns—whole pages at law firms devoted to SDA cases, settlements that set records, cases involving multiple family members over multiple generations, academies with long strings of cases, on and on.

As I kept talking about everything I learned on social media, my direct messages exploded. In the worst possible way I was no longer the solitary ex-SDA. Everyone, it seemed, had a story to tell: how their church-employed family members had been threatened with dismissal if a child pressed forward with a sex abuse charge; how they themselves had been pressured not to talk about an abusive incident because it would make *them* look bad; how they had tried to press charges, but when the legal process got around to interviewing the perpetrators, the church couldn't find them because they had mysteriously disappeared to the mission field, and Church administrators somehow had no way to find or communicate with them. There were pastors' wives who had been pressured to look the other way and had been shunned when they sought a divorce. There were the kids who had been forced into conversion therapy—and molested as part of the "therapy." It seemed like virtually everyone knew someone who had been either a victim or a perpetrator within the church.

When my DMs on Instagram and TikTok got too full and too disorganized, I established an email address. I began to appear on podcasts, talking about the epidemic of child sexual abuse in the Adventist Church, and I began interviewing survivors, which brought even more survivors to my inbox. I started two simple lists: one of all the publicly available cases, arrests, and prosecutions of known Adventist offenders, the other a private file containing everything from the previous document but also every whispered "nobody believed me" story related to each entry, every "they all knew but he never got held accountable" tale, every "I reported it and nothing happened" account.

Predictably, as social media brought me in contact with hundreds of survivors and I spoke out more and more, it also brought many violently defensive church apologists, angry Egg White fans from all over the globe, who denied there was any truth in what I said. They insulted and ignored the victims, championed the perpetrators, and accused me of lying and working for the Devil (or *those Catholics*). Every day there was a fresh deluge of random church members harassing me and discounting everything I said. They simply could not believe such a horrible problem existed within their beloved church because they, personally, had never heard of it.

I couldn't blame the confused and defensive members, mostly; they were self-righteously defending what they thought they knew to be true because no one in the church had ever talked to them about it. Individual churches and schools, the regional conferences, and the General Conference had never addressed any of its dark history cohesively and publicly, leaving loyal attendees ignorant. They railed at me aghast, confused, and frantically grasping at tired scripts of denial and disbelief.

But I wasn't listening to them.

I was listening to Dr. Z's rage.

I was listening to *my* rage.

And I was listening, waiting to hear from those who actually knew what was true, those who *had* heard all of it. Those who were not confused, who were not flailing around. I was listening to hear something, anything, from the Adventist Church. I was listening for its administration—the conferences, the leadership, the organization as a whole—to finally speak up.

Unlike their followers, they did not make a sound.

They would not defend anything.

They were smugly, utterly silent.

43

On impulse, I drive several hours out from LA to visit my parents, hoping for a clarity I can't define. I feel I am finally at a point of resolution. I am not sure what my plan is, but I know I need to visit them before I can move forward.

In their current house Dad has two spaces that are his—I guess we've mostly always had two for him: one common-ish room always pretentiously called "the library," and one sacred room strictly off-limits—Dad's office. They have both always been pretty much the same, filled with religious reference books, Bibles in different translations and languages, vast collections of classical history volumes, and, oddly, several sets of the complete works of Ellen G. White.

I am met with a familiar sight when I walk into the library: on every surface stacks of books, the top one always open, with reading glasses, a highlighter, and pens nearby. I open the book closest to me—Ellen White, of course, obsessively underlined and highlighted, some of which has faded from previous run-throughs and been refreshed. Sophia and I were each gifted an entire set of her works—several dozen small-print books bound in oxblood, a kind of bonded leather, with gold imprints—when we were baptized around the age of twelve. At eighteen I exultantly threw mine into a dumpster on a weekend home from college only to discover with icy chills that they had somehow found their way back into my room a year later. Shaking with fear, I gathered them up again and threw them violently into another dumpster behind a bar, daring them to resurrect themselves and return to my shelves a third time dripping with Jack Daniels and cigarette ash paste. Years later my sister casually mentioned that her set had disappeared after she moved into my room when I left for college. With great relief, I assured her that they were by that time fast friends with Jim Beam and Johnnie Walker at the bottom of the Berrien Springs dump, but they had shortened my life by several years when I thought it was *my* set resurrected.

I lean closer, flipping through, examining random sentences: "It is a sin to speak impatiently and fretfully or to feel angry— even though we do not speak . . . it is a sin to doubt. The least unbelief, if cherished, involves the soul in guilt, and brings great darkness and discouragement . . . How important that we teach our children self-control from their very infancy, and learn them the lesson of submitting their wills to us . . ."

I am overwhelmed with revulsion and fury at the pure cruelty, the heavy *stupidity* of her words. I remember arguing as a young teen with my dad: "Why did there have to be sin?" His answer was that there had to be a contest of good and bad. But why did there have to be a binary (even though I didn't know the word at the time)? There didn't need to be such a simplistic face-off, a good and a bad. If there was an all-good, omnipotent God, he could have made everything all good, right? Oh, but then we wouldn't have free will. But who cares? Do children with cancer get to exercise their free will? If you don't know there's another option than happiness, there's just happiness, right? Isn't that better than innocents suffering? Plus, how is it free will anyway if God commands you to obey and love him or burn in Hell?

I didn't understand how my brilliant father could be so narrow, so stuck. Why he couldn't think outside the box in any way. I force myself to stare straight into that stifling box, the badly-packaged, stiffly bordered idiocy: a poorly written, plagiarized pastiche of the lunatic social, spiritual, and health obsessions of the Victorian era, bound in dozens of burgundy volumes, spewed out by a hallucinating, brain-damaged charlatan, and promoted by a power-hungry coalition of sanctimonious white men for nearly two hundred years. How did my supposedly intellectual father fall for this? How did he construct from these awful books the windowless fortress of theological certitude in which he trapped us all and imprisoned himself, continually pasting those revolting pages over his private wounds and public sins all these years?

How could he believe this horseshit?!

It occurs to me that maybe he doesn't believe it. Maybe all of the repetition, the devout reading and rereading, is a futile effort in *trying* to believe it. The books on the walls, floor, and tables are perhaps defensive padding, a layer of supposed proof he can point to, evidence of what he so desperately needs to believe in order to redeem himself. Rooms upon rooms of books published by Review & Herald in our various houses in various decades in various states—spiritual cocoons lined with leather-bound soundproofing, theological swaddling to protect him from the siren call of truth, of questioning, of reckoning, of critical thinking. Maybe he is simply wrapping himself in those billions of printed pages like a million little tinfoil hats to guard his brainwaves from the things that don't make sense.

The fact that my entire developing childhood—and that of my parents, and their parents—was dictated by a church obsessed with controlling sex and guided by the harsh commands of a dour, joyless fraud suddenly makes perfect sense. Even today it has all come down to sex as it always did. For my father. For me. How could it not, with that background?

I drove down here thinking I was going to tell my dad I've been talking to Dr. Z for over a decade, that she is an amazing person and I have learned so much from her. I thought I would show him how she has opened my eyes to church dogma fucking me over and illustrate how it has messed him up as well. I wanted to ask about his own possible abuse as a tiny child perpetually younger and smaller than all his classmates, living with strangers and locked away in boarding schools his entire teen years. Is that where it all started?

But I don't need to do any of that. I don't need to ask or say any of that.

Because I know now where it ends.

If this were a movie, we'd be wrapping it all up here with just such a cathartic scene, with bonding and confessions and crying and hugging and a bright future of no more secrets. But I have already confronted him. Dr. Z has already confronted him. We will get nothing further. Making a scene with my father will accomplish nothing but exhaust me and hurt my mother. Again.

I turn my attention to her—the beautiful young bride in a picture on the wall, dimpled and sparkling, on the cusp of claiming that glorious promised land of 1950s female existence, marriage, only to have her betrothed quit his career path, drag her from her life as a spoiled Adventist doctor's child into pastor-appropriate poverty and extreme fundamentalism, and betray her love with the most horrific infidelities. The fragile, innocent girl who ended up in a quicksand swamp of pain and hypocrisy—the person among us who was hurt the most—has, in turn, hurt the rest of us the most because of it. Our whole family has suffered in so many ways through my mother's suffering. Meanwhile, the enigmatic perpetrator—my dad, the bad guy—continually inspires us and makes us happy. He enchants, educates, and amuses everyone.

It is not fair.

It is so, so cruel and unfair.

But so is life. Anyone who says differently is selling you something. Like religion.

I am overwhelmed with deep sadness for these humans: for my father and mother. In this awful, suffocating religion handed down to them, forced on all of us, smothering our family for generations, nothing and no one ever told us things aren't always right and wrong, black and white. Or that there is no gray, either—that the two things don't meld into some inoffensive semi-color, a bland smoothie of ethical midline perfection. No—they are both there, all the time, in everything, in all of us: good and evil, right and wrong, yinning and yanging and sloshing and slopping all over the place. The Bible and the church lied to us with their simplistic duality, their all-or-nothing morality culminating in, "When in doubt, have faith!" Thousands of years and a gazillion agenda-driven, power-hungry biblical scholars and revisionists couldn't get it as right as Dr. Seuss did in *Oh, the Places You'll Go!* His rhyming "nonsense" was so scorned and forbidden in our house, but it was wiser than any of them: "Life's a big balancing act."

Real life is messy and full of unresolved dualities that must exist side by side. Things are not fair. Things don't work out for the best, and having faith does absolutely nothing for anybody. My family has been so vested for so long in trying to forget our secrets and sins that we have not even seen the need to extend our professed value of forgiveness to ourselves or to each other.

I can't change what my dad did. I can't force him or my mother, or any of the rest of us, to find peace with it. But maybe healing generational trauma can go both ways, not just parent-to-child: I can heal my own pain by letting go of theirs. It takes work, and I'm doing that work. I don't have to feel guilt for the bad things he did, or for the good I experienced with him. I need to stop centering him and his story. Dr. Z got to have her confrontation with him; I can honor that best by continuing to fight the church for other children.

I have unexpectedly found a calling through this whole mess: speaking out against the church and speaking up for the victims. I can help others work through and let go of their pain, too.

Keeping secrets is the only way people in high-control religions can live with themselves, can live with their families. The only way the organization can live with itself.

I am not keeping secrets anymore.

44

I went out for a run before I left. I had been running since my childhood when my runner father began taking my non-runner sister out for jogs to help her lose weight. I invited myself along on their trips around the block, hoping he would notice I was good at this sport, that we could bond over our shared passion for it. Eventually I was told not to go. It was not about enjoyment or sport or bonding, after all; it was about losing weight, and since I didn't need that, I should just stop.

Soon enough, however, I was pursuing the skinny goal too, and so I took up running again by myself. Nobody needed to torture *me* into bodily perfection, thank you very much; I could do that all by myself. But it turned out that I really loved running, and what I took up as another form of self-torment ended up being a salvation. Lately, in finally getting in touch with my body—communicating with it instead of punishing it—I had realized that I was only truly relaxed while on a run. Many of the techniques I picked up as part of healing had begun to help my overtaxed nervous system and disassociation from my body, but nothing, not even sleep, allowed my whole body to let go, to soften, to be free of the clench like pounding one foot down in front of the other.

I took off slowly from my parents' modest subdivision, reversing an old path I used to take from my nearby maternal grandparents' house in the fancy, older neighborhood at the top of the hill. I trotted on the long, paved streets—once simple dirt tracks crisscrossing my grandfather's ranch on which he and my mother would ride their horses.

I had initially been resistant to the idea of generational trauma; it sounded like a cop-out, the idea that multiple lifetimes of damage can actually rest in our bodies now, that our physical beings can manifest inherited psychological issues we are not consciously aware of. I had scoffed at this as a silly excuse to escape culpability for our behaviors, but now that I had peeled back so many layers and gotten a glimpse into my own core, I had to admit many of those strata had been the stranglehold of previous generations transmitted to me.

I needed to process what my body held, all of it, and finally let it go.

Letting my feet carry me forward, I began to catalog how and why my body was constantly at war with itself and how this had been passed down through my maternal line. The complete denial of my right to control my own body and personhood through a complex array of family and church mandates had manifested itself in many overt negative outcomes over the years, but the destructive cycle hadn't started with me.

I knew my great-grandmother had forced my grandmother to endure painful weight loss massages and starvation diets. In a grossly familiar pattern, Grandma had been tortured into physical perfection but not allowed to benefit from it: on a visit to Paramount Studios, where my great-grandfather worked as props master, her slim legs garnered her an invitation to join the chorus girls. The idea was scorned by her parents, immediately rejected as sleazy and sinful, and this was a decision Grandma resented ferociously her entire life. She had to be slim, but God forbid she enjoy it, use it, or be celebrated for it. Aside from her famous legs, she was a rather homely woman, a fact that was thrown into painful relief when my mother grew up to be extraordinarily beautiful. Falling back into the maternal pattern, my jealous grandmother managed Mom's looks with disdain and ridicule, denigrating her hair and fingernails (Grandma's only other advantages over Mom's

Elizabeth Taylor gorgeousness) and enforcing the curls-at-all-costs mandate that came to haunt my sister and me.

In turn, my mother managed every inch of her children's bodies, from our weight to our posture to our way of walking to the very tips of those hated curls. Every generation had sold the beauty ritual as "Your father likes it when you look this way," and we were no exception, with none of it more stringently commanded or micromanaged than on Saturday mornings in preparation for church. Our maternal legacy choked us all with a toxic and disorienting, "for your own good" medicine to instill us with the notion that men and God outranked us in sovereignty over our own bodies.

I began to review again the separate bits of church dogma regarding men's rule over women: where those intersected with my family's own deeply misogynistic and manipulative roots, where they were then amplified by school rules and pressures before being passed down and intensified, generation after generation. I had now read about cults and their favored mechanisms of control, two very familiar ones being the dictation of members' eating habits and sex lives, so it all made perfect sense.

I examined the subjective and secretive duality in which my sister and I were raised, which we had to tread like a minefield. Everything held a moral weight, a good-or-bad heaviness: sex, lying, stealing, and murder were on the same list as snacking, clogs, straight hair, and Sonny & Cher Barbie dolls. Beauty was the be-all/end-all in our family, but we weren't supposed to be vain or use that beauty for our own ends. We were supposed to have compassion for everyone, but we also absorbed the unspoken teaching that we were better than everyone else.

Because rarely was anything overtly voiced, explicitly codified—it was simply clearly intended, expected, not discussed, and it would have been vehemently denied if in fact voiced. Sophia and I were left in a constant state of trying to instantly and fully obey without knowing what the rules really were, riding a shifting boundary line opaquely determined and judged by others. We were required to aim for perfection but also to never do or be "too much" as defined by . . . some authority or another, but certainly not by us. Underneath it all, we had the disturbing, skulking feeling that there was something shameful and wrong about the whole setup.

I had lived my younger years in a state of hypervigilance that defied description. It was little wonder that as I grew up, not only did I seek out sexual and bodily pain, debasement, and abuse—everything from bulimia to extreme exercise to sex was an opportunity for self-flagellation—but my flesh itself seemed intent on reinforcing my perception of "sin." I was allergic to almost all metals, which kept me from wearing jewelry, the entry-level Adventist sin. I got violently ill if I tried to smoke pot. I had myriad severe reactions to nearly everything surrounding sex and sexuality: hormones in the pill caused life-threatening blood pressure problems, and I developed painful fibroids around the time I started having sex. And, of course, I broke out in blisters and hives from condoms, from silicone lubes, and from latex and silicone sex toys.

My silicone breast implants had caused the most problems. Within three months of getting them so that I could embody Jesse's ideal of womanhood, I developed several autoimmune diseases. The most interesting of these, alopecia, caused me to lose all my hair—God's "crowning glory" and the fetish object of obedient Christian women everywhere. I eventually had the implants removed, but the autoimmune issues were there to stay, a medical condition contracted from my body fighting to protect itself—by ruining itself.

That fit completely. My body had long been bent on self-destruction to spite my lifelong quest to be pretty, pleasing, and sexy, to feel like a sex object. I had wanted, needed to be that object: it was the only way I felt comfortable. An object is not responsible for what happens to it or what it does. The only way I could both preserve that sense of distance from myself and still somehow lay claim to myself in any way was to abuse my body growing up; later, believing myself unworthy of any self-ownership at all, I gave that power to men. I had never believed in my own right to self. I was everybody's open book, everyone's pawn. I never knew I had a right to create and maintain a boundary, to place limits on how other people could relate to me. This was such a bizarre and foreign concept, one denied me by family, church, and school, that I was even now ill-equipped to define and defend any part of myself that others were not entitled to.

Just like the generations before and within me, rabid fundamentalist Christian patriarchy had presented only two options for womanhood: the madonna or the whore. Always the striver, the overachiever, I had tried both—first whore, then saintly motherhood, then back to whore—and these polarizing identities had continued to war in my body even as I tried to scour them out with limitless abuse.

Enough was enough.

My morning run ended as I passed the grand old gates surrounding my grandparents' former home, and I trotted down the hill toward my parents' more modest one. On the ground was a trampled piece of trash, and I bent to pick it up. It was one of those business cards kind people leave anonymously in public toilets and other random places offering domestic violence help to women.

A final piece of self-forgiveness washed over me, jagged breaths coming as they did in that long-ago run during which I had passed out trying to anticipate my future. My healing had been stymied by one obsessive, self-incriminating thought: How could I have been so stupid? So blind? How had I, an intelligent, educated woman, repeated the same patterns, fallen for the same nonsense—escaped so many times only to fall for another version of the same bullshit?

The dirty, cement-sidewalk-pocked card in my hand gave me the answer, right there: it takes abuse victims an average of seven times to leave their dangerous situation.

I don't know why, exactly, the oft-repeated statistic finally hit me to my core. All those attempts to get out of family and church as a teenager, those decade-long devotions to one man after another, each time thinking I had captured something new and healthy? For whatever reason, I was in this statistic. It had indeed taken me at least seven attempts before I'd found my current, still-shaky freedom.

I'd been retreading the same stupid religious trauma, just without the religion, for almost half a century.

Half a century.

I had left the cult, but not the control; ditched the faith, but not the fear. I had been smothered and silenced by way too many men and way too many of their ideologies and institutions.

The grinding of my life had been a water wheel, the weight of its churning decades constantly scooping and dumping the same stuff, inexorable, flowing over me, rushing back to be revisited. The repeated escapes and entrapments, all the circles creaking, spinning, stringing me out on a medieval torture device—not much further and I will be vivisected..

All those wheels I'd been running on were me: spinning, trampling on myself—churning water, providing energy, grinding grain for everyone else—placating, fawning, serving, balancing, becoming, always to find I'd personally gone nowhere. I just became dizzier and more exhausted than ever before, a bone-splintering exhaustion born of constant nervous overdrive and pandering and propping up. I had lived a lifetime of terror, failure, hopelessness, and betrayal. And in all those previous attempts to get out, I had been fighting not only against what had been put on me directly—against my own comfort levels and my childhood programming—but also against the inherited weight of harm done to previous generations.

The generational treadmill of female misery would stop with me. *I forgive you, Melissa. You knew not what you did. But now you do know, so you're going to hang up your gloves and step out of the ring for good. You will fight this fight no more.*

The God of the Bible—that nasty, capricious, demanding, self-obsessed, misogynistic narcissist—will ruin my family line no longer. No more embodiment of patriarchal demands. No more whore, no more Madonna.

Just me.

Now I could extend that grace, that acceptance, to my parents. I had been raised in circumstances of paralyzing control and required submission, but they had supported and loved me endlessly, without judgment or meddling, throughout my adult life. My mother had been cruel and overbearing when I was young, but now I understood the extreme fear and protectiveness that drove her to it. I could grow beyond and refuse to play into the binaries, fears, programming, shame, and gross oversimplification that had made our world a minefield of either/or, good/bad, black/white. I could respect all their self-contradictions and love them without reservation, even if—especially because—they themselves could not.

My dad was a complicated "sinner" and predator, but one who had unwaveringly supported and loved me my entire life—who wore silly hats for his grandchildren, who quietly slipped checks into my destitute hands when he thought no one was looking, whose laugh was legendary. He was the man who had given me a lifetime of academic bonding, inside jokes, historical lessons, and language aspirations. It was a complicated juggle to maintain space for the things I honored and appreciated about my father, without following the church and family party line and sweeping the bad stuff under the rug because it was too painful. The black/white, evil/good easy judgments of my childhood called at every turn—

particularly as I continued to advocate for victims—and I had to make peace with no peace: there would never be easy answers for me regarding my father.

My mother, whom we had always called "Little Mom," and who was now tinier than ever, had shown me the hugest, most ferocious protective love of any mother imaginable. She never ceased in her obsessive effort to keep us safe from that one huge thing that hung over us all—that she could not understand and did not deserve: the terrible predatory actions of the most unexpected and trusted person. If it could be him, it could be anyone, so, with her limited experience and no outside resources, she resorted to blocking out everyone and everything unknown in our lives. This had made her children's lives extremely difficult, but she had, in the end, succeeded in protecting us from falling prey to a child predator. And she had continued her fierce love and given me unwavering support throughout my adult life, even when she must have cried herself to sleep for decades over my decisions.

I hugged them tightly when I returned—sweaty and drained, but at peace. Finally ready to forgive us all and give up the struggle with the past. My past and theirs. I could finally do it for me, and I could do it for them.

But I needed to go back to one more place.

45

I drive east for hours through the dusty California farmland, from my parents' house to the place of my birth: the drab and dinky town where I entered the world and Dr. Z's innocence left it—to where the whole sordid story started.

I have lived less than three hours away for nearly a quarter of a century, but I have never visited before. I drive through the stench of thousands of cows pathetically mired ankle-deep in their own excrement, something that never ceases to shock me with the cruel neglect of it all. I'm not sure if they're waiting for milking or butchering, but it seems they would equally welcome one or the other to alleviate their misery. I feel our bond.

I go out of my way to stop at the scene of James Dean's fatal car crash, the barbed-wire curve on a two-lane highway in the middle of nowhere between Los Angeles and Salinas, where he had been headed for a Porsche race. Items of trash blown by the wind hang indiscriminately off the fence alongside odd gifts left by fans: a lacy bra, a Pepsi label featuring a pen-and-ink drawing, an empty bottle of Jack Daniels, a mini Bible, a crushed cigarette pack, all faded and tattered by the fierce winds and brutal sun of California inland.

Never much of a Dean fan myself, I am somehow still drawn to this site whenever I pass nearby. There is something about the desolation and tackiness that I find magnetic. You went out of the world right here, *Jimmy Dean, Jimmy Dean*. And I came into the world just over there. Godforsaken places both.

I look at the studio portrait of JD and think of my family's golden era Hollywood connections—men on both Mom and Dad's sides working in and around the industry yet holding such supercilious disdain for it, with their women sequestered far away from that allegedly sordid, morally bankrupt environment. Ah, the irony. *That* world was immoral! Predatory! Sex-soaked and sinful! Yet where did all those sins find and affect my family? Their church.

I get back into my car and drive farther into the valley, the temperature rising steadily. Every farm is garlanded with signs: "Build more dams, stop the man-made drought!" and "Stop dumping our farm water into the ocean!" I pass the pyramids of almonds big as apartment complexes, each nut requiring obscene amounts of that same diverted river water indignantly claimed to be "stolen farm water." It's so fitting that the Adventist Church has established a large presence out here on the scorched-earth turf defiantly maintained by climate change deniers, among the strangled rivers, those bastardizations of "God's creation." An organization known for insisting the world is only six thousand years old and that dinosaurs never existed couldn't be expected to abandon their science-backward stance for the facts of global warming, especially when many of them deliberately celebrate any natural destruction as a sign that Jesus is coming.

By the time I reach my destination, it is over one hundred degrees, and the music choices are soft country, hard country, classic country, Spanish-language country, and Christian country. I stop on the outskirts of town. Like pretty much everything in California, the original character of the place is long gone, surrounded as it is by acres and acres of walled-in communities: baked-biscuit-colored, two-story houses with identical floor plans and three choices of entry hall tile.

I google "hotels near me" and look for properties that are old—as old as or older than I am. I think I should stay at one of the dumpy '60s motels that may have been a long-ago crime scene for my father. I read the reviews for one of them, eyes catching on this entry: "I love the fact the owner doesn't allow child molesters and rapists to rent a room, like Super 8 and Holiday Lodge down the street." How nice that they don't do that . . . anymore. I idly wonder how that particular reviewer came to know that specific information. Is there a handwritten sign taped to the check-in desk: "We do not allow child molesters and rapists . . ."?

And what about those miscreants checking in with their underage charges down at the apparently permissive Super 8 and Holiday Lodge? Do they still pray together with their victims before attempting sex? Do they talk about getting married even while their wives are pregnant?

Do they dangle running away together as a possibility but then turn around and guilt the love-starved juveniles for agreeing because it would land the perps in jail? Do they reassure themselves and their captive audience that relationships like this aren't wrong—cultures all over the world marry women off at pubescence and earlier? Do they promise their prey they will always be together, then drop them cold and move on to their next target? Do they tell the victims decades later, "I knew you'd turn out just fine"?

Most importantly, do they have a whole organization, a whole network of enabling men doing "God's work" who clean up behind them—threatening family members' livelihoods, guilting survivors, hiding the evidence, pressuring the news reporters, discrediting the witnesses –all to avoid sullying the careers and reputations of these hallowed men?

Oh, for fuck's sake.

As it turns out, I can't spend a sleepless night in a decrepit room imagining it to be the same one my father used to defile a child while no one defended her. I thought it would be good closure. I thought it would be cathartic. I thought it would be some sort of full-circle exorcism of the past.

I think it is a spectacularly stupid idea. It is suddenly clear that this is just another masochistic maneuver turned in upon myself, masquerading as attempted healing.

I am not here to marinate in the past.

I am here to let go.

It's been approximately half a century since my family was known here, but I still feel like hiding, so I check into one of the nearby tribal casino hotels. I can't deal with the great white Jesus right now—the white Jesus of my racist family, of missionaries and colonization and settlements and manifest destiny and genocide and all the rest of the Christian superiority carnage and bullshit that has gotten us to where we are as a world. The local Indigenous tribe has its own awful trauma associated with the SDA Church, I am certain, as they do with every abominable denomination in this land, so I feel a connection right now; I feel safe on the Rancheria property.

I check in and change for a run, even though I am still recovering from a broken ankle and incredibly stiff from my time-suspending run at my parents' house, where I was also nursing the ankle.

I don't run. I don't sleep. I don't write.

I don't do anything.

I lie awake into the wee hours, Nikes pointed uselessly towards the ceiling, the stranglehold of my running bra keeping my heart in place.

I stare at the shadows above me, watching as dark turns into light.

I finally get up and go out. It's already hot at 6 a.m.

I start running. Skip-limping, if I'm being honest, but after all, I'm here to be just that. Brutally.

Running is something I've done countless times over my life: thousands of miles, millions of steps. I breathe in, I breathe out. One, two, one, two, one, two. Left, right, left, right. Good. Bad. Black. White. Right. Wrong.

My ultra-running days have been reduced to this—a painful, lopsided trot down a couple of blocks with my brain hammering existential breaking points like a metronome.

It's silly. It's funny. It's *not*. It is.

The place where I was born is right down the street: formerly a humble community hospital, now a glossy, well-financed Adventist Health Birthing Center. I stop in front of the shiny, multistory structure to stand in the New Parent parking area next to a sign covered in bird shit announcing a cheery welcome to moms and babies.

I watch new fathers stroll through the front doors. This is where I first met my much-adored father. Dads weren't allowed in delivery rooms back then, and he hadn't yet gone to medical school, so he would have been just like all the other fathers at that point, I guess, waiting outside for their cigars and big pink "It's a girl!" button pins. It's easier to imagine my extremely class-conscious dad smoking the obligatory cigar than wearing that tacky plastic disk, but I'm grateful for its existence; it's one of the only things saved in my baby book. I guess with everything else going on at the time, Mom didn't have much bandwidth during my babyhood for recording my milestones.

I think again of Dad teaching Dr. Z to drive in our blue Bug and the oft-told story of my birth: Mom forgetting to fill her own car with gas so that they had to turn around and go back for Dad's when she was precariously close to giving birth. I narrowly missed being born in the passenger seat, the doctor rushing in to deliver me in his Hawaiian shirt because there was no time for scrubs.

Scrubs or not, apparently it worked, because here I am.

This is where I took my first breath.

This is where I became me: where the umbilical cord to my mother was cut, where my connection to her overworked nervous system was physically severed. My training at Mom's hand had already begun in utero, soaking into my forming tissues—don't speak up, accept what men do, obey, be pleasing, swallow, suppress, squash, smile. My developmental bath in her roiling stress hormones—my cells dividing over and over in a toxic soup of grief, anger, betrayal, abandonment—had officially ended here. It was up to me from there on to play it all out on my own, over and over for the next half century.

I look around the hospital, watch cars on the nearby freeway. There is hardly anything left of the flat, dry land that used to surround this place. It is now a consumer paradise of restaurant chains with big TVs and all-you-can-eat pasta, a sea of Chili's and Hobby Lobbies, America's Mattresses and Auto Zones.

The whole place is so new and soulless it is hard to feel any connection to anything.

So I drive over to the Adventist church and get out to stand in the broiling, empty parking lot. It is a Sunday—the Devil's faux Sabbath, thanks to *those Catholics*—so I know I will have the place all to myself.

Greasy mirages wobble up from the stinking blacktop. I sit on the curb, sweating. I stare at the church.

It is a vaguely Mission Revival style building with a courtyard. I had clearly pictured steps for some reason, but there are none. I am shocked that there is a steeple with a bell—I don't know of any Adventist churches with bells and steeples, and it seems sacrilegious somehow. It seems vaguely—dare I say it—*Catholic*. It is yet another item on that endless list of wordlessly shamed things that provoke vague but intensely anxiety-producing Adventist disapproval indicating the violation of some rule you aren't really sure existed but are pretty sure has been sinfully breached anyway and it must all be your fault.

Jesus. I am feeling guilty because the church has a bell.

There is an outdoor hallway at the back of the main sanctuary building that leads to a little walled courtyard. It pulls me in. The heat billows around me like a sumo suit, making me self-consciously slow and awkward. I idly wonder how Mom kept her hair so perfect in this God-awful place and this God-awful heat. The thought makes me smile. A little.

I enter the courtyard. I can feel emotion leave me, slipping away, hiding. I tell myself that's okay for now.

I observe things clinically, coolly; I am the only cool thing in this sweltering hellscape. It echoes with the emptiness I knew it would since ironically, as much as they eagerly prepare to give their lives to defend Saturday as God's Sabbath Day of rest, they cram it so full with stressful church duties,and rules and regulations, that Sunday turns out to be the actual, real rest day for Adventists.

The pastor's office door, which opens onto the courtyard, is to my left. I pause, facing it. Did the youth pastor have a spot in there too? I picture Dr. Z eagerly waiting here for Dad to furtively open the door and whisk her in. I picture my mother standing nervously, heavily pregnant with me, hesitating before she knocks, willing there to be nothing going on behind the door that she will have to confront.

I turn and walk on. Beyond the pastor's office, in the center of the courtyard, are doors to the sanctuary. They are locked, like everything else.

I turn back in towards the belly of the courtyard. Its other three walls have doors into what appear to be small classrooms, symmetrically matching each other across the formal square. I walk under the portico to read the tag on the first door: Youth.

My knees do a funny little wobble and I stop. The next door is tagged "Earliteen"—a patently Adventist term for junior high kids.

These two doors. These two rooms.

I sag against the wall between them.

I can see each of the other doors marks off another section for children. Braced where I lean, I can read them methodically, but I cannot move. I scan all the way across over the head of a small cement fawn curled up in the middle of the courtyard.

I make out the first door: Cradle Roll—the SDA moniker for a tiny children's corral. Mom would have taken my sister there before church, sitting with her and posting colorful felt animals in a felt ark on a felt board, marching with her as they sang that they were in the Lord's army, all while her mind and heart raced, wondering what was happening right here in these two rooms behind me.

My emotions refuse to come back, but my body suddenly gives out. There is no drama—I don't collapse, I don't faint. I just watch from above, with slight surprise, as my body sinks and slides down, crumpling into a messy crisscross applesauce on the cement outside the Earliteens.

The baby deer and I regard each other glassily.

I look over at the closed sanctuary doors. In front of them is our little family. My gorgeous mother, greeting worshippers with that sad beauty pageant smile I remember from photos. She is gently cradling infant me, a bow taped to my head to ward off that hint of sinful androgyny. My three-year-old sister stands miserably but obediently by her side in a scratchy polyester dress and a torturously curled hairdo.

And Dad . . . at first, I can't see him, because he is surrounded, as always, by people who want something from him, want to be near him, want *him*. But there he is—the magnetic Marlon Brando of my childhood pictures. The full-lipped, half-crooked smile; the intense and sparkling eyes; the reveling in (while also always appearing slightly embarrassed or taken aback by) being the center of attention.

There is so much pain radiating from that glossy family, all mutely linked in so much confusion and anxiety and fear. And that little sponge in my mother's arms? She is being baptized in it all. Her first baptism.

Her body—my body, now aged and worn—begins to shake.

All those hormones and terrors and stresses and longings—unspeakable sorrow, terror, bewilderment, anger, hopelessness—that we shared, my mother and I, boil up inside me in this space that brought it all into being. Tears well up. Bile comes up.

I look around for Dr. Z.

I feel her behind me, peering out of the Earliteen classroom, willing them—us—to look at her, to acknowledge her publicly just once. Wanting so badly to be part of that golden family that wasn't so golden at all; we had just perfected the practice of pretty pain.

I whisper an apology. I can't change what happened to her, but she has given me the fire, the drive to speak up for others just like her. She has given me a mission. Her guidance and friendship have led me to where I needed to go—to dig all the way inward, down, under, in order to finally dig out and let go. I silently, fervently thank that twelve-year-old girl for it.

And then it finally comes: I start to cry, weird, sticky tears hotter than my cheeks, hotter than the air, hotter than the wavy snakes rising from the stinking blacktop parking lot beyond the courtyard. I want to say something; I want to scream something dramatic, but that is just silly and pointless. Drama is dumb. So I remain sitting, silent-sobbing and dry heaving and choking weirdly, the emotions too convoluted to be assigned just one sound. There, cramped and crisscrossed, I remain for I don't know how long, retching in the echoing square, the concrete fawn and I staring at each other.

I remember my only hunting experience with Jesse, when I badly injured a doe. He laughed. I felt awful. She ran off, and we couldn't find her. She ran miles and miles, life force seeping from her for hours on end. We found her the next day, curled just like the cement fawn, suffering terribly. She didn't even struggle when she saw us approach. She regarded me calmly, sadly, deeply, staring her fate down with dignity and acceptance.

I shot her through the eye.

It was kind and it was cruel and I will never hunt again.

My miles of bleeding out on the run are over, too. "I'm sorry," I whisper to the fawn. "I'm sorry," I whisper to everything. I will no longer do pretty pain.

I watch as my little family fades into the stained glass panel beside the sanctuary door, engulfed by its strangely psychedelic, opaque design. It must oddly distort and obscure the outside world with its manufactured image, seen from only one side from the controlled space within. That seems about right.

I wait.

I wait for something. I don't know what.

Maybe just the energy to stand up again.

I can feel the crinkly, dry tightness of salt tears crusting my face. I realize I am sweating. My skin is crying because I cannot anymore.

But I know now. I can stop chasing my father's long-buried story and move forward. I do not need to confront anyone else. No one can tell me the complete truth about this situation; I will never be able to fill in the picture to my own satisfaction. I can't keep turning to others for direction, nor can I expect a new binary to save me. I must embrace both light and dark and let them slosh around in that terrifying, stomach-churning tug-and-tango that they do. I need to hold them gently, simultaneously within me, embracing this faulty humanity—the good and the bad together, unresolved—and that is a radical departure from what anyone in my family has known.

My quest for the truth about my father has turned out to be a long and convoluted search for the truth about myself, and I have found that. It is not pretty, but it is beautiful.

I am ready to go.

I get up—crumbs of cement embedded in my flesh, blood rushing back into my extremities with a sharp tingle. I make my way slowly out of the courtyard, past the darkened sanctuary with its illusory window, past the locked-up pastor's office.

I limp across the boiling asphalt to my car.

I do not look back.

ACKNOWLEDGMENTS

First and foremost, thanks go to my publisher and editor at Lake Drive Books, David Morris! David's calm and reasoned approach offset my ever anxious, brash-and-thrash mode. I am forever grateful to him and Lake Drive for taking a chance on me and my book and never once trying to tone down the graphic personal details or placate the giant organization I critique. Thank you also to my agent, Dani Segelbaum, who signed me on a half-finished manuscript and a lot of faith. She was unfailingly steadfast, calm, and patient while I procrastinated, freaked out, and sulked, dragging the finished draft stage out into years rather than months.

I would not have met Dani or David without the efforts and support of the marvelous team at Book Pipeline, whose one-of-a-kind contest for unpublished/unfinished manuscripts I was lucky enough to win in 2021. Pipeline Artists goes above and beyond in supporting and promoting their winners; thank you, Matt Misetich and crew, for believing in me and my work.

And thank you to those teachers long ago who believed in and encouraged my writing: Mrs. Collins, my third grade teacher who, when I penned a very mean poem about her, chose not to punish me but encouraged me to write because she said the poem was well done. Mr. Baker—the legendary Bake—whose caustic wit and passion for the English language were unsurpassed, even when lecturing from a prone position on the floor just because he liked the change in perspective. And lastly, Mary Gordon and Christopher Baswell at Barnard College and Columbia University, who listened to my woes, encouraged me, mentored me, employed me, and inspired me, providing that little window to the outside world when I so desperately needed it.

So many thanks to the individual dear friends from various stages of my life who read the manuscript in development and gave invaluable feedback and support: Gayle Billat, Charlotte Hayes, Charity Glass, Steve Catalano, Anita Bryant, Olympia Stone, Margot Magowan, and Jennifer Huber Laugier.

To the deconstruction community—the sub-redditors, the TikTokkers, the tight pod on the 'Gram: You are AMAZING. I learn so much from you, I draw so much support and solace from you.

It would perhaps seem upon reading this book that I do not have any female friends, but nothing could be further from the truth. I have been incredibly fortunate to have several of the most amazing, tight, lifelong female friend groups. None of them appear in this book to any demonstrable extent because they were never even remotely a part of the problem. So a deep thank you to all these dear women:

To Mama Duck and the Ducklings: Jami Bernard, Kate Kemp Griffin, and Anita Bryant. J-MAK was the first and only writing group I have ever belonged to because it is hard to improve on perfection. To the LA Athena Film Festival Lab 2019 film pod: Jane Therese, Mary Elder, Cassidy Louwerse, April Sanchez, Tricia Lee, Nina Kentsis, and our beautiful departed Marquette Jones—and to Melissa Silverstein, Elizabeth Kaiden, and Nitza Wilson, for putting us all together.

To my college roommates and lifelong bestest friends Posy and Margot, who were so instrumental in first opening my eyes to the world beyond my upbringing—a world of feminism and academics, critical thinking and social justice—and who have shown me the unshakable merits of true friendship and loyalty. I love you both so much.

And finally . . . thank you to family.

I start with Dr. Z, who is not technically family, but . . . she is. It is hard to convey the complex and forever enduring gratitude, admiration, and sisterhood I have found for and with you. You are generous and brilliant, funny and fierce.

To my starving-artist patrons/relatives, Bill and Ted, for financial sponsorship, family venting, laughs, and emotional support (thank you, Uncle Bill, for being the only family member brave enough to read the first draft)!

A tearful thank you to my big sister for listening to the most painful (and endless!) rehashing, theorizing, introspecting, and ranting—even when you did not agree—and for supporting and encouraging me to tell my version of our lives anyway. And, of course, for being there since I took my first breath. You are the best big sister ever.

To my other close family members who shall go unnamed here—I am forever grateful for your humor, your warm and steady objectivity, and your ability to slow things down and get to the heart without the hysteria I usually bring to everything. Much, much love.

Saving the best for last, my biggest debt of love, apology, support, and thanks goes to my children. To the stepchildren I once had and treasure still from the regretful distance that I, alone, am responsible for; and to my natural-born children, who are my sole reason for existing. You have proven over and over, from tiny childhood into adulthood, that you are wiser, kinder, more insightful, more tolerant, and more broad-minded (and often much funnier) than I will ever be. You are daily, living proof that growing ethical, responsible, caring, and compassionate humans does *not* require religion. I am so honored to share my life with such brilliant beings. I love you endlessly and forever.

BIBLIOGRAPHY OF QUOTATIONS

Franklin, Benjamin (Author), and Japikse, Carl (Editor). *Fart Proudly: Writings of Benjamin Franklin You Never Read in School.* Frog Books, 2003.

White, Ellen G. *Child Guidance.* Review and Herald Publishing Association, 1954.

White, Ellen G. *An Appeal to the Youth.* Seventh-day Adventist Publishing Association, 1864.

White, Ellen G. *Selected Messages, Book 2.* Review and Herald Publishing Association, 1958.

White, Ellen G. *An Appeal to Mothers.* Seventh-day Adventist Publishing Association, 1864.

White, Ellen G. *Gospel Workers 1892.* Seventh-day Adventist Publishing Association, 1892.

ABOUT THE AUTHOR

Melissa Duge Spiers is an award-winning essayist, screenwriter, and speaker on topics of religious abuse and resilience, utilizing her online platforms (TikTok and Instagram @theglorywhole) to raise awareness and help others find healing. Her memoir *Holy Disobedience* won the 2021 Book Pipeline Unpublished Nonfiction Manuscript prize, with excerpts featured in *The Huffington Post*. Melissa's writing has appeared in magazines nationwide, and she's a contributor to *Take the Fruit: An Anthology of Religious Trauma*. She holds a BA in English Literature from Barnard College and is based in California.

ABOUT LAKE DRIVE BOOKS

Lake Drive Books is an independent publishing company offering books that help you heal, grow, and discover. We champion books about values and strategies, not ideologies, and authors who are spiritually rich, contextually intelligent, and focused on human flourishing. We want to help readers feel seen.

If you like this or any of our other books at lakedrivebooks.com, we could use your help: Please follow our authors on social media, subscribe to their newsletters, and tell others what you think of their remarkable books.

www.ingramcontent.com/pod-product-compliance
Lightning Source LLC
LaVergne TN
LVHW040045080526
838202LV00045B/3495